DIRECTING DRAMA

BY THE SAME AUTHOR

Speech for the Speaker (Angus & Robertson)
Speech Training and Dramatic Art (Pitman)

JOHN MILES-BROWN

Directing Drama

**ILLUSTRATED WITH PLATES, DIAGRAMS
AND CHARTS**

U.S. DISTRIBUTOR
DUFOUR EDITIONS
CHESTER SPRINGS,
PA 19425-0449
(215) 458-5005

PETER OWEN · LONDON

ISBN 0 7206 0557 1

PETER OWEN LIMITED
73 Kenway Road London SW5 0RE

First published 1980
© 1980 John Miles-Brown

Printed in Great Britain by
Bristol Typesetting Co Ltd
Barton Manor St Philips Bristol 2

To Barbara

ACKNOWLEDGEMENTS

Thanks are due to the following for their kind permission to quote from published works and articles:

Tania Alexander, executor of Moura Budberg's estate, and Davis-Poynter Ltd for Moura Budberg's translation of *Three Sisters* by Anton Chekhov; A. D. Peters & Co. Ltd for *An Inspector Calls* by J. B. Priestley; The Bodley Head Ltd for *Building a Character* by Konstantin Stanislavski; Jerzy Grotowski and Odin Teatrets Forlag for *Towards a Poor Theatre* by Jerzy Grotowski (© 1968 Jerzy Grotowski and Odin Teatrets Forlag); Penguin Books Ltd for Una Ellis-Fermor's translation of *Hedda Gabler* by Henrik Ibsen, and for John Wood's translation of *The Imaginary Invalid* by Molière; Eyre Methuen Ltd for *Loot* by Joe Orton; the executor of Luigi Pirandello's estate for *The Rules of the Game,* translated by Robert Rietty; and *Theatre Quarterly* for the quotation by Paul Scofield in Chapter 9.

CONTENTS

ILLUSTRATIONS

Plates

Plates are reproduced by courtesy of the following: 1, 2, Bernard Watson; 3, 5, TABS (Rank-Strand Electric); 4, The Festival Theatre, Chichester; 6, The Crucible Theatre, Sheffield; 7, The Royal Exchange Theatre, Manchester; 8, The Victoria Theatre, Stoke-on-Trent; 9, Camera Press Ltd; 10, John Vere Brown; 11, David Farrell and the Royal Shakespeare Company; 12, 13, Zoe Dominic.

Figures in the Text

Figures are reproduced by courtesy of the following: pages 43, 46, TABS (Rank-Strand Electric); 44, Theatre Projects Consultants Ltd; 48, Architects, Denys Lasdun & Partners; 49, 51, Jerzy Grotowski and Odin Teatrets Forlag (© 1968), drawings by Jerzy Gurawski.

Introduction

Theatre is an ephemeral art. The text of a play remains in print, but the performance, in terms of live theatre, lives only in the memory of the audience and is finally extinguished. Criticism, film or video tape of a stage play can impart a flavour of what it might have been like to be present at a certain performance, but it cannot recapture the immediacy and the feedback between cast and audience, what Bernard Levin calls 'the electricity of the theatre', that makes each enactment unique. When the performance is over we are left with only the memory of a complex series of thoughts and images that may have moved us to laughter, tears, anger, disgust, uplifted us, made us think, subjected us to a variety of thrills, or allowed us to escape into the staged world of the dramatist.

The making of theatre is the work of the director and each director, inevitably, to a greater or lesser extent, imprints upon the finished production his personal style – for he has translated the text from page to stage, using his chosen cast, production team and technical facilities to present his particular interpretation of the play.

In recent years we have become accustomed to what is called 'director's theatre', where gifted directors with strong personal styles make their treatment of the play the outstanding feature of the production. The director virtually becomes the star, a function formerly monopolized by the leading player, and his treatment sometimes makes more impact than the work of the cast. There has, however, recently been a reaction to this trend; indeed, Peter Hall has suggested that it is perhaps time the actor returned to a more dominant role in the theatre. The Actor's Company, founded by Ian McKellan in 1972, has this view in mind and chooses the director it feels is most suitable for the company, which is the reverse of the usual procedure.

Nevertheless, it is the director, as artistic overseer, who is finally responsible for creating the dramatic image that burns on in the memory, sometimes for years, when most of the minor details of a production are forgotten. These persistent images usually contain the essence of the interpretation of the play. Let me give some examples. There was that moment in Peter Brook's 1949 production of *The Dark of the Moon*, when William Sylvester as the Witch Boy returned to his kindred spirits. He was sitting on the ground centre stage, tense and still in the moonlight, aware of the pull of the witch world calling him back to freedom. In a long silence we were aware of the intensity of his inner conflict, then, triggered by a sound of the night, we saw him released from human bondage. He suddenly relaxed – seemed to lose weight, spun like a top, froze suddenly then leaped to his feet and was in that instant transformed to a creature of another world, a wild thing – evil. It was splendid acting, but the total impact was engineered by the impeccable sense of atmosphere, movement and timing set by the director.

Another occasion was at the end of Act IV in Laurence Olivier's production of Chekhov's *Three Sisters* at the Old Vic in 1969, when the sound of the military band escorting the departing regiment, which has made itself part of the texture of the lives of the sisters, grows faint in the distance. Chebutikin, the failing Army doctor, sits with the paper and hums softly to himself, 'Tara-ra-Boom-di-ay. . . . *(Reads the paper.)* It's all the same, all the same. Nothing matters.'

The whole delicate arrangement of timing, stillness, lighting and sound levels captured the mood of that final moment when the three sisters standing together face the prospect of a life the suffering and purpose of which they do not understand. From this ostensibly gloomy prospect was distilled an image of great dramatic power and beauty.

Finally, I remember a moment during the Moscow Art Theatre's performance of *The Cherry Orchard*, at Sadler's Wells Theatre in 1958. In Act II, during the conversation at sunset by an old shrine, there is a pause, and, according to the script, 'a distant sound coming as out of the sky, like the sound of a string snapping, slowly and sadly dying away.' Of all the various productions that

I have seen of *The Cherry Orchard* this was the most moving. The entire theatre was stilled by a quiet, but unearthly, sound that seemed to herald irrevocable change. The masterly handling of this brief moment reflected the quality of direction of the whole play.

There is no one 'correct' way to direct a play. A study of the methods of the outstanding directors of the past and the present reveals very clearly that each director has his own personal approach which arises from his view of the function of theatre in society, the particular play in production, the technical facilities at his command, his individual aptitude as the interpreter of a text, his manner of working with a cast and gauging the reactions of the audience for whom the play will be staged. Directors evolve their methods of work over a period of years and also modify their approaches from play to play. Directing is learned by directing plays and there is no substitute for that practical experience. Experience as an actor or stage manager or working in the production team, as well as having an insatiable appetite for theatre, seems to be the usual way in which a director develops his sense of dramatic imagery and gains an understanding of the practicalities of theatre.

This book attempts to show methods of approach to the job of directing drama and the various factors that must be considered from the time of choosing the play to the opening performance. Whether working on a professional or amateur basis the director has to strive constantly for the highest standard possible within the prevailing conditions. It is this constant striving for perfection – perhaps, in the end, unattainable – and the realization of a particular interpretation, in an art form where compromise is inevitable, that creates the challenge and compulsion of directing.

1 *Some Directors Past and Present*

Surprisingly, it was only about one hundred years ago that theatre programmes indicated that one person (then called the producer) was responsible for directing the production. He might also have been the leading actor, stage manager or the author, so his work was not exclusively that of directing and therefore it would not be easy for him to have had the single-minded concentration, interpretation and objectivity that we expect from today's directors. Today the producer is the person with financial and managerial responsibilities. The director is responsible for all artistic aspects of the staging of productions.

The present-day function of the director has, of course, been influenced by and evolved from the work of a succession of dynamic men of the theatre during the past century, who have brought new vision to the task of staging drama. Directors, designers and theoreticians have constantly experimented with new forms of drama, theatre shapes, styles, techniques and methods of interpretation, in the quest for the ideal synthesis of text, actor, setting, and audience that makes theatre.

One of the first of these was a German, the Duke of Saxe-Meiningen, who had married an actress, Ellen Franz. From 1874 until 1890 he ran his own company, with Ludwig Chronegk as his stage manager and later as producer. The aim was an integrated company paying great attention to accuracy of detail in settings and costumes, which were designed by the Duke himself. All aspects of the production were subject to his firm discipline (Stanislavski regarded him as justifiably despotic) in which actors, costumes, realistic settings, sound effects and stage movement were blended in intensive rehearsals into a unity of pictorial and dramatic effect. The European tours of this co-ordinated and disciplined company had great influence on the theatre. They played at Drury Lane in 1891.

The French director, actor and manager, André Antoine was influenced both by the work of the Meiningen Players and by Emile Zola's doctrine of naturalism. He founded the Théâtre Libre in Paris in 1887, and presented the work of Ibsen, Strindberg, Brieux and Hauptmann among others. He regarded the influence on performance of a facsimile stage as highly important, as this 'real' setting would determine the movement and influence characterization; the environment becoming a dramatic element in its own right. Later he founded the Théâtre Antoine, presenting the plays of the younger dramatists, thus foreshadowing the work of George Devine at London's Royal Court Theatre in Sloane Square.

The Meiningen Players' attention to details and veracity also influenced Konstantin Stanislavski, co-founder of the Moscow Art Theatre with Vladimir Nemirovich-Danchenko in 1898. Although Stanislavski died in 1938 his work as actor, director, teacher and writer provides us to this day with a method for training the actor and guiding the work of the director. His famous 'System' is still the basis of most drama training, although it may not be necessarily referred to as the 'Stanislavski System'. In America, 'the Method' propounded by Lee Strasberg and Elia Kazan at the Actors' Studio, New York, is an adaptation of the Stanislavski System and has produced some remarkable actors.

Stanislavski was responsible with Nemirovich-Danchenko for the famous Chekhovian productions at the Moscow Art Theatre, which are, of course, theatre history. In his early days Stanislavski devoted great attention to external naturalistic details, such as properties, furniture, costumes, sound effects and lighting. He would work out extraordinarily detailed production notes with plans and sketches to realize his visualization on the stage. Everything was exactly delineated; movement, business, voice, mannerisms, and so on. In later productions, however, he revealed that he regarded external truth as insufficient and worked for an inner truth in the actor's performance – psychological realism. The quest for these two forms of truth, internal and external, led him over the years to formulate his System, which is not, it must be firmly stated, a rigid process, but a method of approach, aspects of which good actors have always used instinctively.

Stanislavski was one of the first to suggest that the duty of the director was to seek in the work of the dramatist a 'ruling idea', or super-objective, which would be the main factor guiding the interpretation of a play. Gradually he placed less emphasis on external naturalism and more on the development of the actor's character. His three books, *An Actor Prepares, Building a Character* and *Creating a Role,* are a trilogy planned to show the training of an actor. The first deals mainly with the psychology of the actor, the second and third books have more emphasis on technique. His autobiography *My Life in Art* was published in Russia in 1924, while *Stanislavski Produces Othello* (1948) and *Stanislavski Directs* (1954) concern his work as a director.

Adolph Appia, a Swiss designer and theorist, urged in his book *Die Musik und die Inscenierung* (1895) that the director should become a despotic drillmaster synthesizing the elements of scenic production and dominating the actor. He compared him to the leader of an orchestra. He advocated symbolic and anti-realistic staging, suggesting the atmosphere of the location rather than faithful naturalism. He also worked out a system of stage lighting to create atmospheric effects. His ideas were intended to be applied to operatic and Shakespearian productions rather than plays written in the naturalistic style.

Edward Gordon Craig, the son of Ellen Terry, was a director, designer and theorist. His influential book, *On the Art of the Theatre* (1911), proposed the idea of the director being the supreme power, an alchemist of the theatre, using the actor as a kind of marionette. Rather like Adolph Appia he stressed the importance of creating a setting that would be non-representational, an environment that would reflect the style, accommodate all the scenes of a play and by means of colour in lighting affect changes of mood and atmosphere. This type of setting for an all-purpose acting environment is frequently utilized by designers today – especially in productions of classical drama.

Another director who moved away from naturalistic representation was Jacques Copeau. In 1913 he devised for his theatre company, the Vieux-Colombier, a permanent acting environment with a variety of levels, entrances, steps and a central raised platform. Scenery was reduced to a minimum. This method of staging was designed to accommodate a style of acting in which the movement and the diction of the actors would reflect the dramatic rhythms of the play with the precision of a musician playing notes of music. He regarded the dramatists' text and the direction of it as two stages of a single operation and felt that the director as a specialist had a duty to be completely faithful to the text. To strengthen the actor-audience relationship he removed the proscenium arch and footlights, creating an open-staging form.

An Austrian actor, director and manager, Max Reinhardt, was renowned for his highly spectacular productions with masterly crowd movement. He was a creator of grandiose effects, using all the theatrical means that he could command. For his production of *The Miracle* at Olympia in 1911, the interior was transformed to look like a cathedral. His productions used the widest range of techniques. Reinhardt felt that each play demanded its own style and mode of staging in order to bring it fully alive. He prepared his productions in his *Regiebuch* (director's text) in meticulous detail with diagrams and elaborate notes for all concerned, so that the completed *Regiebuch* was a master-plan covering every aspect of the production: rehearsals, staging, costumes, characterization, lighting, music, and even at times audience disposition. For Reinhardt the text was not of prime importance, as for Jacques Copeau, but just one of many factors he could use to create a theatrical experience. The actors were treated in much the same way as he manipulated the text and technical facilities, so that voice, gesture and movement were all subservient to the master-plan. However, it should be remembered that he was also a skilful director of intimate chamber dramas in the 300-seater Kammerspiele and the Kleines Theatre, which demanded great subtlety of treatment. He was, incidentally, the first to run a school to train directors.

A contemporary of Stanislavski, Vsevolod Meyerhold, was a member of the Moscow Art Theatre from 1898 until 1902. A Russian actor, director and theoretician noted for his experimental work, he sought upon the stage 'a symbolic expression of life'. He relied heavily upon improvisation, rather than having the play meticulously documented in his director's copy, as, say, Stanislavski did in his earlier productions. Meyerhold moulded both the text and the actors to create a vigorous theatrical event. He wanted his actors to move in a stylistic and acrobatic manner and have considerable mimetic skills, with lightning reflexes and absolute control. To this end he developed in his Theatre Workshop a method of movement training for actors which he called 'bio-mechanics'. The actor was basically a super-marionette as advocated by Edward Gordon Craig.

Bertolt Brecht (1898-1956), was a German poet, dramatist, director, theoretician and Marxist. His theatre company, the Berliner Ensemble, was, and still is, devoted to the presentation of his own plays, for each of which he prepared a *Modellbuch* (an elaborate version of the director's copy of the play) complete with a record of all moves, timing and photographs of productions. His theories of drama, about which he wrote copiously and revised from time to time, are reflected in his production techniques. The Alienation Theory (*Verfremdungseffekt*) was a way of making the audience constantly aware that they were sitting in a theatre watching a play about which they were required to think, rather than be carried away on a wave of emotion or sympathy for a particular character. The actor 'demonstrates' his role rather than immerses himself in it, as Stanislavski wished, so that the audience will not wax sympathetic and lose their ability to criticize the situation. Actors may wear masks, or step in and out of character to become a narrator for a moment. Placards carried by the cast may announce the title, time and location of a scene; slides and film clips may be projected; the mechanical apparatus of staging may be in full view; there may be a small band on stage to accompany a burst of song from the actors, who are not to be mellifluous singers, but can put a song across with a gutsy rawness that inclines one to listen to the words rather than wallow in the sound. Brecht's form of theatre, which he called Epic Theatre, is a series of self-contained scenes designed to appeal to reason, not that emotion or empathy could be entirely excluded, for the poetic element in Brecht's dramatic writing does not always keep an audience 'alienated' in the way he wanted. The Berliner Ensemble visited London in 1956, shortly after his death, and his methods of staging were perhaps more influential than his political form of theatre. Brechtian staging methods are now fairly commonplace and have been used notably by Robert Bolt in *A Man for All Seasons*, John Osborne in *Luther* and in musicals such as *Godspell* and *Cabaret*.

Antonin Artaud (1896-1948) was a French playwright, director (he founded the Théâtre Alfred Jarry with Roger Vitrac) and theorist. His book *The Theatre and Its Double* (1938) has, belatedly, in the last twenty years, inspired many directors to attempt to put his theories into practice. Artaud wanted the theatre to move away from psychological realism to the realms of myth and magic. It was to be a theatre of spectacle, using emotive effects, spectacular lighting, beautiful costumes, rhythmical movements, masks, giant effigies, strange music and sounds, cries and groans. Dialogue was to be minimal and delivered in an incantatory manner. He wanted the theatre to be a place where the audience would be subjected to a visual and auditory experience that would liberate forces in the subconscious and by so doing have a cathartic effect.

Peter Brook and Charles Marowitz together presented a Theatre of Cruelty season, using Artaud's methods, at the LAMDA Theatre in London in 1964. Those who attended the performances, drawn from a variety of material, will not easily forget the impact of Artaud's play *Spurt of Blood*, although it lasted only three minutes. The audience were seated in the acting area and the action took place on and around the steeply raked auditorium, so all the action was directed down at the audience – the victims, as it were. Bizarre characters shouted, groaned, cried out, ran, contorted, conflicted in an agony of spirit and then with an almighty shriek a huge hand about twelve-foot-long thrust out above the heads of the audience with blood-red streamers that spanned the theatre vibrating from the fingers. The image was indelible. Elements of Artaud's Theatre of Cruelty ('cruelty', by the way, may be construed as akin to ecstasy combined with the terror and awe of primitive ritual, and in his letters answering objections to the term, published with his book, he explains that he used the word 'cruelty' in the sense of an appetite for life – a cosmic rigor) are to be found in many exotic theatrical productions today, where spectacle is supplied by scenic effects, flashing lights, bizarre costumes, masks, pyrotechnics with explosions, flashes, smoke, incense and audience bombardment by quadrophonic sound.

Lindsay Kemp's production of Oscar Wilde's *Salome* was a very clear example of this – where the performers spoke the little dialogue there was in an incantatory manner as well as using the other techniques mentioned above. We were drawn into an exotic and bizarre world of mime, dance, throbbing music, incense, multi-coloured lighting and fantastic costuming where the impact was sensory and emotional rather than cerebral and approached

what is called Théâtre Total, a technique used at times by the
French director Jean-Louis Barrault.

Jerome Savory's Grand Magic Circus Theatre Company uses
rather similar techniques. When this French company brought
Robinson Crusoe to the Roundhouse they used elements of Defoe's
story to stage a rumbustious spectacle, in-the-round, in which
almost every possible tactic was employed to enliven their interpretation, the loneliness of man. The audience were packed in
tightly, some sat on chairs, some on the floor and many were
standing. From the start, the performance literally exploded in
and around and over the audience with deafening music, garish
lighting, acrobatics, tightrope walking, fire eaters, audience con-
frontation, strippers, song, dance, shouted dialogue and unlimited
vitality.

In 1953, Joan Littlewood took over the Theatre Royal, Stratford East, and forged a brand of theatre the basis of which was a
company improvising around a text. The final results, which were
invariably dynamic, often incorporated song, dance and Brechtian
techniques such as simple functional settings and actors stepping
in and out of character. She excelled in presenting the meatier
aspects of life in a broad and flamboyant style that made one
come out of the theatre, if not necessarily uplifted, enriched and
enthused. Her greatest achievement to date, is, I believe, *Oh What
a Lovely War,* in which with Charles Chilton and the company
she devised a show depicting the patriotism, courage and futility
of World War I. It is a musical on the lines of a pierrot show
using Brechtian techniques, including a lighted indicator totting
up the mounting casualties as the show proceeds. The context of
a musical threw into relief the waste, madness and heartbreak of
war.

Jerzy Grotowski, a Polish director, has his own theatre laboratory in Wroclaw. It is subsidized by the state and has the status
of Institute for Research into Acting. He works with a small
group of actors and the results of his work are occasionally shown
to audiences of often not more than forty people. Performances
are based on Polish and other classics 'whose function is close
to the myth in the collective consciousness'. The performances
have about them an intensity and anguished concentration. The
acting area is one of extreme simplicity – in fact he calls his type
of theatre a 'poor' theatre. The use of voice and movement by the

actor are considered all important and portray moods and emotions that have the style of what might, at times, be described as a religious frenzy. The actors produce vocal tones and movement patterns that are quite removed from those experienced in conventional theatre and perform as though they are in a trance. In his book *Towards a Poor Theatre*, Grotowski acknowledges that this is a theatre for an elite. The film *Theatre Laboratorium* issued by Contemporary Films shows vocal and movement training and performance.

Another influence on contemporary British theatre has been the removal of censorship in 1968. Under the office of the Lord Chamberlain plays could be banned, subject to the removal of references or actions that could give offence. Usually these were of a religious, sexual or violent nature. If you look at the rear of many play texts printed just before the removal of censorship you may see a list of words and actions that must be omitted in performance. However, immediately censorship was removed some directors felt that they had to get in on the act and nude scenes seemed to be almost obligatory for a short time, not because the text demanded it, but to produce a fashionable *frisson*. Now that the novelty has worn off, violence, sexual acts and four-letter words (the most common of which was launched into the ether by Ken Tynan, the then dramaturge of the National Theatre, during a BBC Television broadcast) are usually to be found only in productions where they are thought to be essential to character or theme. Impact is not necessarily enhanced by saying, showing or doing what has previously been taboo. One has to leave something for the imagination of the audience to work on and, as in a radio play, imagination can sometimes beggar an attempt at scenic reality.

These then are some of the influences that have shaped the approach to directing today. In his work the director has behind him the theories, experiments and practice of the Meiningen Players, André Antoine, Stanislavski, Adolph Appia, Edward Gordon Craig, Jacques Copeau, Max Reinhardt, Vsevolod Meyerhold, Bertolt Brecht, Antonin Artaud, Joan Littlewood, Charles Marowitz, and Peter Brook, who like Jerzy Grotowski and Artaud before him is seeking a language that will transcend the barrier of national languages. In Brook's production of *Orghast* at the Persepolis Festival in 1971 Ted Hughes devised a text for him that attempted to do this. Brook is one of the most brilliant present-day directors. As Ken Tynan says, he has an uncanny way of skilfully manoeuvring actors, in an almost hypnotic manner, into carrying out his intentions.

In this brief survey of the diverse approaches of some directors during the past century, what emerges, apart from the individuality of style and varied aims and methods, is the single-mindedness, indefatigability and in some cases fanaticism they have brought to the quest for the unattainable – the amalgam of play, cast, setting and audience that is perfection.

Let us now take a look at some of the qualities that the contemporary director may need. Perhaps the first essential is to have a fairly broadly based understanding of human behaviour and relationships and an awareness of the complexities of life, because drama normally deals with people at a point of crisis. This means that you need to have an interest in psychology and what it is that makes people behave as they do. Then you need a well-developed sense of visual and aural imagery, so that when you read a script you can, in your mind's eye, see and hear the play as a staged performance. You need a sound knowledge of present-day theatre techniques, so that you know that your ideas are capable of being developed by your cast and are realizable in practical terms by your designer and stage management. Similarly an understanding of the history of drama, staging, costume and social customs and an appreciation of music are necessary. It is essential to be able to establish an easy working relationship with people and to inspire your cast to be truly creative, experiment and extend themselves to the limit. You have, by one means or another, to create the atmosphere and conditions in which this can take place. A sense of humour is vital, as is a sympathetic insight into the psychology of the actor, but at the same time you need discipline and control. It may seem strange to talk of discipline in the theatre, but it is an attitude towards the work and is an internal thing in actor and director, not superimposed. As a director you will find that your role will, at times, range from the artistic and organizational to being a drama instructor, diplomatic listener or oracle.

You need to be able to analyse a play to:

a. Find its theme or, as Stanislavski referred to it, the ruling idea or super-objective.

b. Observe its intricacies of plot, sub-plot and sub-text.

c. Locate its dramatic climaxes.

d. Understand the style of the play and the characters and their relationships.

e. Visualize how it can be most effectively staged and moved, with sets, costuming, décor, lighting, sound effects and music.

You also need to have an understanding of the actor's technique. Most directors have at some time been actors and this experience gives them an insight into the various ways actors work.

A useful exercise is to see different productions of the same play and observe the way each director has handled it. You will find that one of the problems in analysing productions is that the better the direction the more difficult it is to be absolutely certain of the exact degree of responsibility of each contributor, for a first-class production is shaped with such harmony that the individual elements, clearly visible in a poor production, fuse into the unity of the dramatic experience.

2 The Drama Company: Areas of Responsibility

The director must be familiar with the structure of the organization that backs up his work of interpreting and staging a play. The performance on the stage is supported by specialized teams that may be divided into two main functions: *artistic*, under the guidance of the director, and *administrative*, under the General Manager or Administrator.

A drama company is usually governed by a Board of Management, which normally appoints an Artistic Director to assume responsibility for the actual functioning of the company, choice of plays for presentation and maintenance of standards. In an amateur company the chairman of the Theatre Management Committee or Drama Society may also be the artistic director.

The artistic director and his administrator must work together to ensure smooth functioning of the organization and to check that the cost of mounting productions and running expenses do not outstrip income.

DRAMA COMPANY ORGANIZATION

The Producer The Producer is the board of management, drama society or individual with the financial and promotional responsibility.

Artistic Functions

Artistic Director The Artistic Director controls production policy, directs major productions and may have one or more

24

Associate Directors.

Designer

The Designer works closely with the artistic director designing productions, supervising construction and painting. He may have one or more Design Assistants. The designer may also design the costumes, if not, he will nevertheless be in close consultation with the Costume Designer, as the costumes are an integral part of the overall design.

The Acting Company

The actors are either cast for specific roles in a certain production or 'play as cast' in a permanent company.

The Production Manager

The Production Manager is responsible for costing productions and supervising and co-ordinating the work of all the departments backstage.

The Stage Manager

The Stage Manager is responsible for all the physical aspects of staging a production. He makes up the prompt copy of the play, showing actors' entrances, exits and moves, as decided in rehearsals by the director, together with all cues for curtains, lighting, effects, music, flies, warning bells, etc. He orders costumes, wigs and furniture. To his Deputy Stage Manager and Assistant Stage Managers he delegates such jobs as properties, prompting and the dozens of tasks a production entails. An efficient and imaginative stage manager, who works without fuss and organizes his team in a businesslike way is an inestimable asset to any director.

The Lighting Designer

The Lighting Designer is a specialist and in consultation with the director designs the complete lighting set-up. The Lighting Technicians rig and operate the lighting. In a small company one person may take responsibility for all lighting work. Some directors prefer to design their own lighting.

The Sound Technician

The Sound Technician records and plays back all music and effects on tape. In a small company an assistant stage manager may do this work.

The Master Carpenter

The Master Carpenter, with his assistants, constructs the setting from the designer's scale drawings. He also, with the stage manager, supervises the erection of the completed setting.

The Wardrobe Mistress

The Wardrobe Mistress has charge of all costumes on hire, as well as those made for individual productions. At the dress parade and at the dress rehearsals she and her staff note any repairs and alterations that have to be made and keep costumes in good condition during the run.

Administrative Functions

The Administrator

The Administrator has responsibility for budgets, control of expenditure, payment of accounts, the legal aspects of drama presentation, including theatre regulations, and all business matters.

The Public Relations Officer

The Public Relations Officer arranges for printing and display of posters, handbills and hanging cards. He designs the layout of programmes and arranges printing. He contacts the press, radio and television with advance information about anything newsworthy and puts advertisements in the press. He runs the mailing list and generally stimulates interest in the theatre and its presentations.

The House Manager

The House Manager is in charge of the reception areas, bars, buffets and cleaning staff. He may have responsibility for checking ticket money with the Box Office Manager and money from sale of refreshments. An important part of his job is to welcome the audience and ensure that the auditorium is in readiness with usherettes in attendance with programmes.

The Box Office Manager

This is a job needing patience and tact. The box office is the first contact the members of the audience have with a production – apart from publicity. It therefore is essential that there is a sense of welcome. Curtness at the box office can dull the edge of an evening's entertainment, while a friendly reception can at least predispose the audience to start the evening in a receptive frame of mind.

These are the people who create the environment within which you, as director, present your production to the audience. You are dependent on them and you need their full support, therefore the establishment of a pleasant working relationship with all concerned is essential.

The range of artistic and administrative tasks outlined above represents the basic set-up for most theatre companies. However, it is wise to remember that the conditions under which the director works vary enormously. In an established company there will, of course, be a resident production staff, headed by the production manager, to carry out all your staging requirements, but in very small companies such as fringe, itinerant groups and some amateur companies, there may perforce be some doubling up of jobs. The producer may also be the director and the cast may have some responsibility for stage management, wardrobe, lighting and décor; or in an *ad hoc* situation you, as director, may have to form a production team from scratch.

3 *The Script*

Before proceeding further it is necessary to consider the raw material that the director shapes into a stage presentation – the script. Weeks of work will be invested in the production by you, your cast, the production team and business management – so, firstly, it is essential to make a choice that can be cast and staged satisfactorily and will appeal to the appetite of your particular audience, and secondly, and this is most important, it must excite your creative instinct strongly enough to impel you to direct it.

This means that you will be looking at plays from a particular point of view – the director's point of view and with the above criteria in mind. On the other hand, of course, you may have been invited to direct one particular production and therefore you may proceed immediately to the stage of thinking about the text for production purposes.

As you study the text there are certain points you must clarify for yourself, so that when you come to your pre-rehearsal preparations you will be sure of your line of approach for the whole production. This analytical stage usually means that you will be reading the play through as many times as are necessary to gain a thorough grasp of the play, with, hopefully, a breathing space between each reading to mull over the impressions you have received.

The first reading will be, perhaps, just to enjoy the play and to observe the main action, leading characters and general style. In subsequent readings, in which it may be useful to make notes of things that strike you as important, there will be various points that you will want to resolve for yourself. They are:

THE THEME

What is the theme of the play as a whole? What does the play say? What is it about?

As director, you must know towards what conclusion you are to steer the production, otherwise it will drift and be an incomplete, and therefore unsatisfying, experience for the audience. Stanislavski talked about the 'through line of action' of the play, which gives continuity and guides the actors from the beginning and leads to the super-objective or main theme. Stanislavski regarded the 'through line of action' as being constituted from the small units of the play, each having an objective or theme and combining to lead on to the super-objective, that is the main theme or, as he sometimes called it, the ruling idea of the play. Harold Clurman calls it the spine of the play, a term he took from Richard Boleslavsky, in which the smaller units of the play may be compared to the vertebrae, which together form the spine. So, call it the theme, message, super-objective, ruling idea, or spine of the play, as you will. These terms convey the author's conscious or, sometimes, unconscious meaning. You may find that some plays do not have any clearly definable theme – they may work in terms of theatre by creating moods, atmosphere and situations or revealing characters. The realization of these can therefore be your theme. In a light comedy, for example, the success of the whole play may depend upon revealing the verbal wit, the foibles of contrasting characters, the twists of the plot, the exuberance of the situations and getting the audience to relax, laugh and thoroughly enjoy themselves.

STYLE

What style or dramatic convention does the author use to put across the content of his play? Formerly it was thought desirable to have plays neatly classified into types of drama that conformed to certain literary requirements, such as comedy, farce, tragedy, melodrama or other conventions. In the present day the range of drama has widened to include all aspects of human life and many plays do not fit snugly into a classification or indeed may embrace two, three or more styles. For example, Joan Littlewood's

Oh What a Lovely War has elements of a comedy, a documentary, a musical, a political play, a tragedy – you may discover other styles in it. One of the greatest and most influential plays of recent times, Samuel Beckett's *Waiting for Godot* is at one and the same time comic, tragic and philosophical. A play does not necessarily conform to what were regarded in the past as set conventional patterns. Today an author may simply describe his play as 'a play', or say nothing, leaving it to the director, cast and audience to decide its genre. However most plays do veer nearer one mode than another. For those not already familiar with the range of dramatic conventions it might be helpful to point out the characteristics of certain styles.

Naturalism is a style of presentation in which the dialogue, situations, acting, production and settings attempt to show, as Zola put it, 'a slice of life'. The audience watches the action through the 'fourth wall' of the setting, represented by the open prosccnium arch, with the actors ostensibly unaware of them, although, of course, voice, speech and movement are meticulously rehearsed to be heard and seen in all parts of the auditorium. The content of plays presented in a naturalistic manner can, of course, range from comedy to tragedy.

In *comedy* the humour arises, in part, from characterization revealing the foibles of human nature. Comedy usually demands a deeper sense of characterization than is normally found in farce, but the success of comedy, as with farce, depends very much upon subtlety of timing. (Examples are *The Government Inspector* by Nicholai V. Gogol; *Enter a Free Man* by Tom Stoppard; *The Philanthropist* by Christopher Hampton.)

The *comedy of manners* satirizes manners and social behaviour. The style is usually brittle and the dialogue has a scintillating quality. Comedy of manners makes considerable demands on the actor's technique. (*The Relapse* by Sir John Vanbrugh; *The Importance of Being Earnest* by Oscar Wilde; *Hay Fever* by Noel Coward.)

Many musicals could be regarded as *romantic comedies,* where in a mood of fantasy, love and adventure may be combined with song and dance routines. Some of Shakespeare's plays have the qualities of the romantic comedy. (*Twelfth Night* by William Shakespeare; *The Enchanted* by Jean Giradoux; *Ring Round the Moon* by Jean Anouilh.)

In *farce* we watch stereotyped people caught up in the mechanics of a fast-moving plot that has been carefully constructed to manoeuvre the characters into situations that are for them embarrassing, but for the audience hilarious. As the farcical plot is a contrived situation, the action has to be fast-moving, well timed and acted with considerable technical skill to prevent the audience dwelling on any improbabilities. Maintaining a façade of calm and respectability amid calamitous occurrences, often of a sexual nature, is the mode of farce. (*Hotel Paradiso* by George Feydeau and Maurice Desvalliers; *The Magistrate* by Arthur Wing Pinero; *Loot* by Joe Orton.)

Greek classical tragedy deals with the decline of a noble character from fortune to misfortune culminating in death. The progression to the downfall of the protagonist is occasioned by an error of action which leads inexorably to destruction. The language is elevated, being in verse, and the chorus, who establish a link with the audience as they comment on the action, sing and dance.

The performances of the four plays, three tragic and the fourth a bawdy satyr play, on the same day in the Theatre of Dionysus, below the Acropolis in Athens, were in the 'Golden Age' a matter of religious and civic observance. The catastrophe of the downfall of the protagonist should have the effect of *catharsis,* inducing, by a savouring of pity and terror, a cleansing of the emotions.

Although the original notations of music and choreography are lost, each year in the summer, you may see, in the Theatre of Herodes Atticus, next to the ruins of the Theatre of Dionysus, performances of the Greek classics, tragedy and comedy, which give an insight into the handling of the plays and the engineering of stage devices, such as the *deus ex machina.* (Examples of tragedies are *Agamemnon* by Aeschylus; *Oedipus Rex* by Sophocles; *The Bacchae* by Euripides.)

In *Shakespearian tragedy* the protagonists are of noble stature (Hamlet, a prince; Othello, a noble Moor, general of the Doge's forces; Lear, an aged king; and Macbeth, a general in the king's army) marked by the Shakespearian tragic flaw of character that brings them to eventual destruction. As Hamlet says in Act I, Scene iv,

So oft it chances in particular men,
That, for some vicious mole of nature in them,

As, in their birth, wherein they are not guilty,
Since nature cannot choose his origin,
By the o'ergrowth of some complexion,
Oft breaking down the pales and forts of reason,
Or by some habit, that too much o'er-leavens
The form of plausive manners; that these men,
Carrying, I say, the stamp of one defect,
Being nature's livery, or fortune's star,
Their virtues else, be they as pure as grace,
As infinite as man may undergo,
Shall in the general censure take corruption
From that particular fault: the dram of evil
Doth all the noble substance of a doubt
To his own scandal.

The complexity of the characters, subtlety of themes and quality of language give a finely textured drama that probes the nature of humanity.

The protagonists of *modern tragedy* (some would question if tragedy in terms of drama is possible in these times) have not the distancing effect of time or high estate that gives the aura of legend and nobility to Greek and Shakespearian tragedy. Three modern plays regarded as being in the tragic style are: *Death of a Salesman* by Arthur Miller; *The Shadow of a Gunman* by Sean O'Casey; *Huis Clos* by Jean-Paul Sartre.

Melodrama nowadays infers a sensational type of drama portraying strong emotions and employing music, lighting, and stage devices to heighten the effect. The situations are relatively unsubtle, without the texture of plot found in more realistic plays. The characters also tend to be stock types representing a set point of view, again without the characterization in depth found in realistic drama. In Victorian times melodrama was common theatrical fare. (*The Bells* by Leopold Lewis; *Sweeney Todd* by George Dibdin Pitt; *The Silver King* by Henry Arthur Jones.)

Expressionism is a form of theatre which attempts to show inner psychological conflicts rather than represent outward appearances naturalistically. Characterizations and settings tend to be symbolic, with extravagant playing and striking décor making a strong visual impression in order to put across the dramatic point forcefully. Frequently there is a mood of great stress and

B

sometimes a nightmarish quality. (*The Ghost Sonata* by August Strindberg; *R.U.R.* by Karel Capek; *The Adding Machine* by Elmer Rice.)

The *Theatre of the Absurd* was not an organized movement, but rather the manner in which some dramatists in the 1950s expressed their views of the world. In 1942 Albert Camus, in his essay 'The Myth of Sisyphus', used the term 'absurd' to describe the purposelessness of an existence out of harmony with its surroundings. Similarly the drama of the Theatre of the Absurd reflects shock at the absence of stable systems, beliefs and values. If the world is irrational then the Absurd dramatists reflect it. The form and content break away from the style of the well-made play, with its clear-cut theme, plot, characters and conclusion based upon set values. In its place we find ourselves confronted by irrational situations often presented in the form of poetic images, with the mocking of convention and language. The plays often free-wheel into a world that is a mixture of Monty Python, the Marx Brothers, Lewis Carroll, nightmare and Franz Kafka. The best of them have a firm philosophical undertone and apart from, intentionally, disturbing the conventional they are frequently hilarious and macabre while at the same time establishing their own stageworthiness. (*Waiting for Godot* by Samuel Beckett; *The Chairs* by Eugene Ionesco; *Professor Taranne* by Arthur Adamov.)

Epic theatre is a style of theatre evolved in the 1920s by Erwin Piscator and Bertolt Brecht. The plays are written in short self-contained scenes and the object is to present social and political issues in such a way that the audience, instead of becoming emotionally involved with the fate of the characters, can sit back and arrive at a judgement of the case as presented. This is achieved by what Brecht called the Alienation Effect (*Verfremdungseffekt*) in which the audience is constantly reminded it is in a theatre watching a performance. The actors demonstrate their roles rather than fully embody the character, as in normal naturalistic acting. The action is interrupted by the projection of slides, film clips, actors holding placards and songs sung in such a way that makes you notice their content rather than the beauty of the singer's voice. The singers are usually accompanied by a small band situated on stage with the actors, not hidden in an orchestra pit. Actors step in and out of character as they address the audience or become narrators. Settings are usually simple and the trappings of theatrical machinery such as lighting, scenic devices and ropes, which are normally hidden by the drapes or flats of the proscenium arch stage, are revealed to constantly remind the spectator that he is in a theatre watching a play. Brecht wanted the removal of theatrical illusion to keep the audience alert and critical, but nevertheless strove to keep his form of theatre as entertaining as possible. The use of Brecht's methods of staging is now fairly widespread.

These then are some of the more common styles of drama. There are various permutations and combinations; to attempt to list a full range would be pedantic. Each text has its own distinctive style and set of values and every production of the same text is subject to the interpretation given to it by its director and cast. Furthermore, the interpretation given by a director to a text can give an emphasis that appears to change its style.

THE CHARACTERS

In your preliminary study you must satisfy yourself of the following:

a. Who is the main character?

b. What is his driving force or objective? (What makes him tick?) You can probably answer this by asking, What does he want?

c. What are the relationships and attitudes between the main character and the other characters?

d. Who are the other characters? What are their objectives and their relationships with each other?

You need to be able to see each character as a person with a background, a present state of mind and some sort of objective which motivates the line of action of the character through the course of the play. Further, you must observe if and how the characters are changed during the action of the play. Every character, if it is a fully written character, no matter how small the part may be, has some sort of objective or urge that makes him a credible stage presence.

THE PLOT

The plot is the arrangement of the situations in the play by means of which the dramatist has manoeuvred mutually reacting characters to reveal the action, tensions and final resolution. There may be one or more sub-plots which link, in greater or lesser degree, with the main plot. An example of excessive attention to plotting can be found in the well-made plays of Eugène Scribe (1791–1861) and Victorien Sardou (1831–1908) in which the plot, engineered with mechanical precision, made everything appear over-contrived. The famous farces of Labiche, Feydeau, Pinero and Ben Travers rely upon the highly ingenious manipulation of situations to give the momentum for arousal of the 'constant laughter' of well written, well directed and well acted farce. It is important therefore for you to have a clear image of the structure of the play so that you can see how the plot enables the characters to reveal themselves and the theme to emerge. In thinking about the plot, observe how it operates. Is it sequential – unfolding from A-Z, in a straightforward style? Does it use the flashback technique? Does it use the 'onion skin' technique in which bits of information are fed to the audience until eventually the complete set-up is revealed? Is it in short self-contained scenes, as in Brecht's Epic theatre? Observing the structure of the play should also help when you are preparing your rehearsal call sheet, so that you can plan to rehearse scenes and characters in the most convenient order.

Some plays, of course, have the minimum of what you could call a formal line of plot. The characters talk, tensions build, characters react, we receive a sequence of impressions, souls are bared, moods are created, but no marked sequence of events occurs and the characters remain much as when we first met them, as in Harold Pinter's *No Man's Land* for example. The power of the drama lies largely in savouring moods, images, timing, the language and tensions.

DIALOGUE

Dialogue in drama has a very precise function. As you read the play through, the dialogue should be giving you the information you need to direct the play. The language, as a whole, should reflect the style (convention) of the play to inform you whether the mood is, say, one of comedy, tragedy, melodrama or absurd; whether the treatment is naturalistic, with colloquial or regional dialogue, or moving away from naturalism into the realms of romanticism or fantasy or a classical style, where the use of verse form, with rhythm and imagery, reinforces the content and imparts a universality not easily conveyed in vernacular styles.

The dialogue should reveal the individuality of the characters and show the way they think and react towards other characters. As the dialogue carries the action forward it should (apart from stage directions) indicate time, place, occasion, mood, and variations of tempo, and should reflect the climactic moments of the play. The dialogue may also possibly range back to before the time of the present action to fill you in with details necessary for the understanding of the events of the play.

SUBTEXT

The words spoken may also cover the meaning of any unspoken subtext, where what is said hides or is different from what is really in the minds of the characters. When looking at a text it is important to probe, to attempt to discover implications beneath the surface meaning of the dialogue. Is the dialogue meant to be taken literally, or is there a wealth of meaning and feeling behind the words spoken that can be indicated by subtle use of voice, timing, gesture or business that will give the dialogue a richer texture and reveal the character in greater depth?

Inflexions, timing, gesture and movement can completely change the meaning of a printed sentence. 'No,' can be inflected, timed and acted to mean 'Yes', or vice versa. As a director you must be sensitive to the possibilities of interpretation.

In this extract from Act II of J. B. Priestley's play *An Inspector Calls,* the Inspector is questioning Mrs Birling about the death of a girl. He is showing Mrs Birling a photograph of her.

INSPECTOR [*taking back the photograph*]: You recognize her?
MRS BIRLING: No. Why should I?

This could be played as a completely honest denial, but if it was it would nullify the character of Mrs Birling, who has in fact recognized the girl immediately. Therefore, although she says, 'No. Why should I?', her voice and timing and possibly some subtle gesture should reveal to the audience that behind the words of her denial there is a wealth of feeling: a mixture of pride, apprehension, an intense dislike of the girl and disapproval of the Inspector.

In Chekhov's *The Cherry Orchard* in Act IV, almost at the end of the play, Lopahin, the self-made man and purchaser of the estate, has agreed to meet Varia to propose to her before she leaves for good. Varia comes into the room and pretends to search for something in the pile of luggage. Their mutual embarrassment makes them talk of anything but the purpose for which they have come together. After a short series of hesitant speeches somebody outside calls to Lopahin. He instinctively seizes this as an excuse to avoid forcing himself to propose to Varia and quickly leaves the room. Varia, left alone on the stage, weeps. Not one word of Chekhov's dialogue mentions the thoughts that are in both their minds. It is the subtle revelation of these unspoken thoughts that can make this one of the most memorable scenes in the play.

In Edward Albee's *A Delicate Balance,* towards the end of Act I, Harry and his wife Edna arrive unannounced at the home of their old friends Tobias and Agnes. Their arrival might at first appear to be a social call, but they are deeply frightened – of what they cannot say – and they need the comfort of their old friends. Under the text, behind the things said and done lies this fear and the stresses it places on relationships. It permeates the whole play. What cannot be stated in words must be substantiated by a mental imagery that gives the sense of fear Harry and Edna carry with them a credibility. This is the problem the actor and director have to solve together – the fear may be of the void of death, the emptiness of a life-style, a final realization of dispensability, a need for physical contact or a lack of sustaining faith.

CUTTING THE TEXT

Cutting dialogue, especially with authors whose pens run away with them, is, on occasions, necessary. It must, however, be done with great care to maintain the completeness of the action and the fullness of character. There are many plays that are most difficult to cut without causing complications. Some of Ibsen's plays, for example, are so textured that a line of dialogue may contain important information not just from actor to actor, but also for the audience about past events, the characters themselves, the locale or the dramatic situation. Generally Ibsen writes so 'tightly' there is no redundant dialogue at all; even what appear to be generalized pleasantries are an essential part of the text conveying information.

4 *The Audience*

The Drama's laws the drama's patrons give
For we that live to please, must please to live.
DR SAMUEL JOHNSON

The audience is an essential component in making theatre. Each production is undertaken as an offering to a particular type of audience. Without the presence of an audience the purpose of a production is lost; for the purpose is the reaction of the audience to the play and cast and the reaction of that cast to the response of the audience. Theatre is a creative interchange that is clearly observable in the laughter, silent absorption or applause from the audience; also the quality of the performance itself is influenced by the degree of appreciation and attention of the audience. The audience and cast are evaluating one another during the progress of the play. The audience are responding to the play and the playing; the cast are responding to the audience's response to their playing. Responses flow backwards and forwards all the time. Casts, during and after a performance, comment on the quality of an audience. One almost tangible quality of an audience is how much it can give in the way of rapt attention or quality of laughter and this can guide the playing. A danger in this last point is that some casts may be less sensitive to the full attention of an audience than to the more limited aim of obtaining their laughter and in a basically serious play may be tempted to 'play for laughs' rather than as rehearsed. One has to envisage something like an electrical circuit, in which actor responds to actor *through* the audience and it is this inclusion of the audience in the flow of thought and action that makes possible a fully satisfying theatrical experience.

Audiences have different appetites; they attend certain plays and theatres to savour a certain type of theatrical fare – it may be to be morally uplifted, reassured, thrilled, to savour romance, be shocked, titillated, sexually aroused, to gain psychological and philosophical insights, to escape from dull routine or even just to be a member of an audience and savour and share the process of making theatre. If you ask people why they attend the theatre you may be given a mixture of the above reasons, or indeed some may not be able to pinpoint the particular satisfaction they obtain. The director must, during the time of preparation and rehearsal, plan everything as he would wish his future audience to see and hear it. The director *is* the audience until the first performance. Therefore it is imperative to consider the audience at all planning stages and rehearsals.

It is interesting to compare audiences one sees at theatres with a reputation for drama of a certain calibre with others offering different fare. The National Theatre's and Royal Shakespeare Company's audiences are usually a different mixture from those attending, say, a Haymarket or Drury Lane musical. Again smaller companies operating in pubs, clubs and cellars will attract a different type of audience from those for the frothy comedies of Shaftesbury Avenue. A regional repertory company may, on the other hand, because the choice is limited to one or possibly two theatres, have an audience representative of a wider range of the population, often with an apparent preponderance of older people. It is sobering to realize that it has been calculated that not much more than 2 per cent of the population are regular theatre-goers.

Remember that a parochial audience is unlikely to wax enthusiastic over a very sophisticated or *avant-garde* play and that an unsubtle play presented to audiences used to more demanding fare is not likely to get a good reception. There is a place and an audience for all types of drama from the lightest comedies to the most intellectually demanding of plays. The experience of release in laughter from a very simple comedy, for example, may not be shared by the academically minded, but it fulfils a valuable social function that is not to be scorned. It is a way of viewing life that is as valid for its particular audience as the savouring of the metaphysical anguish of Beckett is for his audience. Audiences shop around for theatrical fare which they feel they might enjoy at that moment. Therefore in choosing a play, the type of audience you are likely to attract in the region of your theatre must be given consideration. The co-operation of the audience is imperative for the making of successful theatre. They must feel that the content and style of your presentation gives satisfaction, so that they can return to the stage the quality of appreciation that is necessary for the full experience of theatre. Appreciation is inevitably modified by cultural background, temperament and the average age of the audience. Audiences do have to be encouraged to appreciate drama that is new to them or alien to their expectations.

As a director you will want to present a complete range of drama. Drama deals with all aspects of life, some of which may not appeal to people with limited views. When Ibsen's *Ghosts* was first performed in London in 1891, the critics and audiences were unaccustomed to the frankness and allusions of the play and seemed quite unaware of its spiritual qualities. William Archer, the translator, critic and dramatist, collected some of the outraged comments which he published in the *Pall Mall Gazette* on 8 April, 1891. Here are a few of the press reactions: 'Noisome corruption' – *The Stage*; 'Gross, almost putrid indecorum' – *The Daily Telegraph*; 'A repulsive and degrading work' – *The Queen;* 'Just a wicked nightmare' – *The Gentlewoman;* 'Garbage and offal' – *Truth.*

Yet on seeing a production of *Ghosts* today one is impressed by the honesty of Ibsen's theme and the sober strength of his play. Conversely, plays that were very successful in their day may later appear naïve or dull and require very skilful direction to make them interesting to a contemporary audience. As a director you should be aware that even what you regard as your finest offerings will not necessarily meet with the appreciation that you feel is your due. A dramatic criticism that is full of unstinting praise is very rare indeed and even the most favourable have their reservations. Press criticism does not always accord with audience reactions – so tumultuous applause from the audience does not mean that all critics will like the play and production. Alternatively, a play that gets a tepid reception from an audience may receive favourable reviews. Again, productions that have been panned by the critics sometimes enjoy long runs. So, be warned, you won't please all of your audience all of the time, for as Jean Giradoux said, 'The audience hears and composes as it pleases, following its own imagination and feelings.'

5 Theatres and Stages

A theatre is a place where a theatrical experience is created by the interaction of actors and audience. It may be in the open air, as with the ancient Greeks or the contemporary Regent's Park Open-Air Theatre, or a purpose-built or adapted structure, but in all cases the most important factor is the manner in which the actors and audience can communicate. That is, firstly, the audience hearing, seeing and being physically near enough to the action to feel fully involved with the business of the stage and, secondly, the actors being able to project voice and speech and reveal the action in terms of movement to the audience and at the same time be sensitive to the response of that audience.

It follows that the size, shape and relationship of the acting area and auditorium are very important indeed. Each theatre has its own characteristics, which predispose it to be more suitable for some types of performances than others. A subtle naturalistic drama would be too intimate and be almost lost in a large theatre that might satisfactorily accommodate a musical. Members of the audience furthest from the actors might miss the nuances received by those sitting near the stage, but if you enlarged the scale of playing to project to distant members of the audience those near the actors would probably be put off by the exaggerated use of voice and movement. It is necessary, therefore, to think in terms of the scale or amplitude of what has to be fed to the audience. If you stand on the stage of a theatre and look out into the auditorium you should become aware of the way in which your production must be tailored to the characteristics of the stage and auditorium. The size and shape of the theatre need to be considered carefully when planning a production.

Perhaps one of the most interesting features of contemporary

43

theatre design has been the realization of the need for the theatre building to bring the actor and his audience into the most favourable physical relationship, not only in order to facilitate the interchange between the acting area and the auditorium, but for the audience to be able to generate an identity and awareness as an audience that transcends the individuals composing it. The experience of being an audience is perhaps most manifest at a football game or boxing match, where the audience surrounds the action and comments audibly on the proceedings. In drama this awareness of being an audience is clearly felt in the Odeon of Herodes Atticus in Athens, which holds 6,000, or at Epidaurus, which can seat 14,000 people, where the audiences sweep in a huge semi-circle round the acting areas and spectators are aware of each other, not just because they can see and pick up reactions from one another, but because they are almost in contact, side by side, on the stone seating. The shapes of the tiered auditoria also focus the attention of the audiences sharply down on the acting area.

As plays are usually written with a particular form of staging in the mind of the author, normally that form of presentation best serves the play. Perhaps I should hastily add that most plays are adaptable and many plays that were conceived for, say, the proscenium arch stage work satisfactorily in other forms of theatre, such as in-the-round or on thrust or open stages, but there is usually one shape of theatre building that suits a play best. A farce, for example, written with a proscenium arch stage in mind and needing six doors, from which the cast make quick entrances and often even quicker exits, might be impossible to stage in-the-round where scenery of that nature has no place, because the use of doors is essential for the proper functioning of the play. Some recently constructed theatres have been designed to be flexible, so that the staging area and auditorium are easily changed to give proscenium arch, thrust, in-the-round, traverse or other forms of staging.

For example, the Octagon Theatre, Bolton, can be used as an open end stage, thrust, or in-the-round. The Questors Theatre, Ealing, adapts to proscenium arch, thrust, or in-the-round. The LAMDA Theatre can be adapted for proscenium arch, open stage, thrust, in-the-round or, as in the Theatre of Cruelty season, the whole auditorium can be used for staging, with the audience

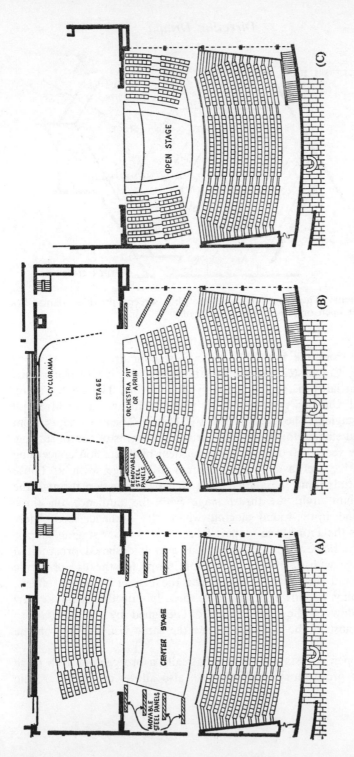

The Leob Centre, Harvard University, adapted to (a) centre stage, (b) proscenium arch stage, (c) thrust stage.

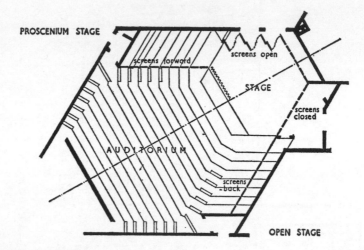

The Mercury Theatre, Colchester. Movable screens provide adaptability for either open or proscenium arch staging.

viewing from the normal floor-level staging area. The Mercury Theatre, Colchester, adapts by adjustable side walls from open (with partial thrust) to proscenium arch staging. The Leob Centre, Harvard University, adapts from proscenium arch to centre and thrust staging. The Bristol Old Vic Studio Theatre adapts from open end staging to either thrust or various forms of centre staging.

A few years ago there was a great deal of discussion concerning the relative merits of the proscenium arch stage, with its house curtain (tabs) and the audience all viewing the action through the proscenium arch, the thrust stage with the audience on three sides, and in-the-round staging where the audience completely encircles the acting area – apart from various other staging shapes. Basically, however, it is agreed that a well designed proscenium arch stage with fly tower offers more scope for the use of scenic devices and thus gives the audience the benefit of scenic effects, which may be flown in and out speedily, together with a view of the flow of the dramatic action designed by the director to enable most of the audience to see the same visual image on the stage.

The open end stage, which is basically a proscenium arch stage with the proscenium arch removed, also allows the use of scenic devices and gives a unified view of the flow of dramatic action. However, any method of staging in which the audience partially or completely surrounds the action prevents the use of scenery the height of which would mask the actors from any part of the audience. In thrust staging, therefore, scenery has to be in the nature of a background to the action and furniture and props set to cause the minimum of visual obstruction. No conventional scenery can be used with in-the-round staging, although I have seen ingenious skeletal frameworks in use that cause the minimum of obstruction. The visual impact usually has to be made by floor décor, suspended items that do not interfere with lantern angles, low furniture and costumes of a quality to bear the scrutiny of an audience in close proximity.

Perhaps the best known British theatres in-the-round are the Theatre in the Round at Scarborough, the Victoria Theatre, Stoke-on-Trent, designed by the late Stephen Joseph, and of course the Royal Exchange Theatre, Manchester. This is a theatre module built inside the Royal Exchange hall. It has three tiers of seating encircling the acting area. It can be converted into a modified thrust stage or a three-quarters round stage. These three theatres are professional, but in-the-round staging is a form frequently used in schools and colleges and has the great advantage of enabling the encircling audience to be very near the acting area, and – important these days – it is an inexpensive method of staging, as everything has to be kept as basic as possible. Also, the proximity of the cast and audience creates an atmosphere of involvement with the action and does not put the demands of projection techniques, that are second nature to the professional, on young amateur actors. However, in in-the-round and thrust forms the actor inevitably has his back to a proportion of the audience and as, apart from voice, the main instruments of communication are the face and eyes, the director of an in-the-round or thrust stage performance has to be extra skilful in his use of movement and grouping to ensure that the encircling audience is getting value for money, without it appearing that the actors are moving too obviously to feed out points and reactions in all directions. Also, both in-the-round and thrust forms need special care in lighting to ensure that lantern angles do not illuminate or dazzle any member of audience.

The majority of professional theatres operate on a proscenium

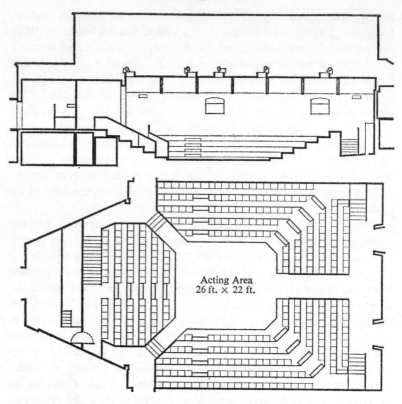

Acting Area
26 ft. × 22 ft.

The Victoria Theatre, Stoke-on-Trent. Theatre-in-the-round.

arch stage equipped with a fly tower; some also have revolving stages, traps giving access from below stage, and means of adjusting the height of the acting area and extending the stage out towards the audience over the area of the orchestra pit or front stalls. In some cases the width and height of the proscenium arch can be adjusted for special productions.

Some theatres built in recent years utilize the form of the thrust stage, with the audience on three sides of the acting area. The best known of these are the Festival Theatre, Chichester; the Festival Theatre, Stratford, Ontario; the Tyrone Guthrie Theatre, Minneapolis; the Playhouse, Leeds and the Crucible Theatre, Sheffield.

The three-theatre complex of London's National Theatre is an architectural achievement that clearly acknowledges the need for staging-auditorium requirements that lend themselves more readily to the demands of the classical and modern repertoire than would a single adaptable theatre. It would be fair to say, in passing, that in designing a flexible theatre a degree of compromise has to be made that means that at least one of the forms (proscenium arch, open end, thrust, in-the-round or traverse) is not wholly satisfactory. The Olivier Theatre is the largest of the three theatres in the complex, seating 1,160 in two tiers and the furthest seat is only 70 feet from the stage. The audience is arranged in a 90 degree arc, rather like a fan, and has a very close relationship with the stage, embracing it and having its attention concentrated on the acting area. This concentration is increased by the rather steep rake of the seating. The open stage and raked fan-shaped seating give a sense of being in contact with the action. There is a large fly tower, the front of the stage can be varied in shape, motorized wagons move scenery swiftly into place from backstage assembly areas and a unique drum revolve of 11.5 metres diameter, split into two semi-circular sections, and also trapped, facilitates speedy scene changes and the working of the repertoire.

The Lyttleton Theatre, a proscenium arch theatre seating 895, has, like the Olivier, the audience arranged in two tiers. The height and width of the proscenium arch are adjustable and the stage itself can be fully raked. There is a fly tower over the stage equipped with a power-operated flying system and motorized scenery wagons can effect quick scene changes from the rear and side stages.

The Cottesloe Theatre is the third theatre in the National Theatre complex. It is a studio theatre and holds up to 400 people, depending on the form of staging used. The studio measures 66 feet by 56 feet and has galleries on three sides. The floor area may be arranged for seating and staging with a considerable degree of flexibility.

Supporting the three theatres are unrivalled facilities for design and construction, costume and wig making, lighting, sound and all technical requirements. The theatres mentioned have, of course, been designed following research, consultation and an awareness of the serious shortcomings of many existing theatres. However,

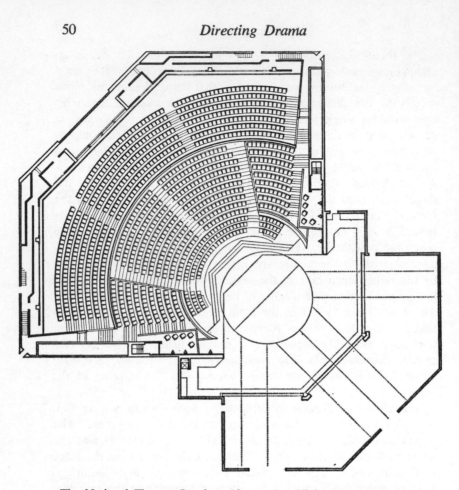

The National Theatre, London. Above: the Olivier Theatre. Facing, top: the Lyttleton Theatre; bottom: the Cottesloe Theatre, adapted for in-the-round (*r*) and end stage (*l*) productions.

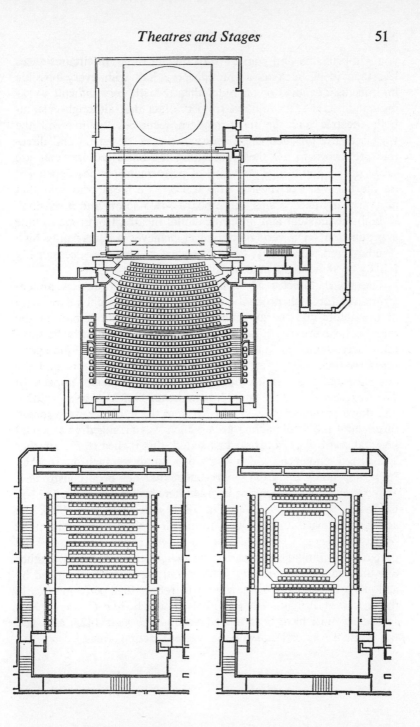

you will probably find yourself directing, at times, in circumstances less than ideal, such as a multipurpose hall with every possible built-in disadvantage or an older theatre with very difficult working conditions. Take comfort from the fact that although custom-built theatres and the most modern technical facilities oil the wheels of the production process and actors, designers and directors are drawn to use these amenities, the basic requirements are fairly simple and a high standard of performance is not dependent on the hardware of theatre. It was Lope de Vega who said that all you really needed was 'three boards, two actors and a passion'. In both the amateur and the professional theatre, from time to time a production on a very tight budget achieves a remarkably high standard and, conversely, lavishly staged productions occasionally fail to be more than mediocre.

The Polish director Jerzy Grotowski normally devises an environment for each production in which the physical relationship of the actors and the audience becomes an essential part of the theatrical experience. In his production of *Doctor Faustus* the spectators were seated at long table-like platforms that were the acting areas, so that there was an intermingling of the actors and the audience and a proximity that intensified the dramatic impact. In *The Constant Prince* the encircling audience looked over a partition and down at the actors, while in *Kordian* the audience were spread throughout the whole acting area, which was arranged as a mental hospital ward. As Grotowski has stated, this is theatre for a rather specialized audience, which may not number much more than forty, depending upon the environment that has been constructed.

When Ariane Mnouchkine brought her theatre company, Théâtre du Soleil, to the Roundhouse in 1971 with their play *1789*, the action took place on raised platforms all around and in the midst of the audience, who were free to sit, or move and watch any part of the simultaneous action that caught their attention. Rather like the audience in Grotowski's *Kordian* they were surrounded by action on all sides. It is interesting to reflect that performances in the medieval Rounds, such as that in which *The Castle of Perseverance* must have been staged around the year 1425, also had the audience spread around the various acting areas.

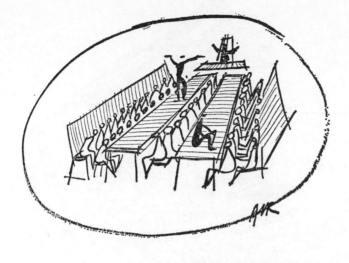

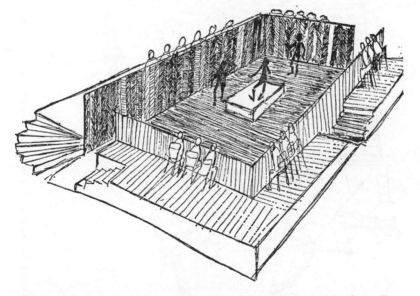

Jerzy Grotowski's staging at the Theatre Laboratory, Wroclaw. Top: Marlowe's *Doctor Faustus*. Bottom: *The Constant Prince* by Calderon-Slowacki.

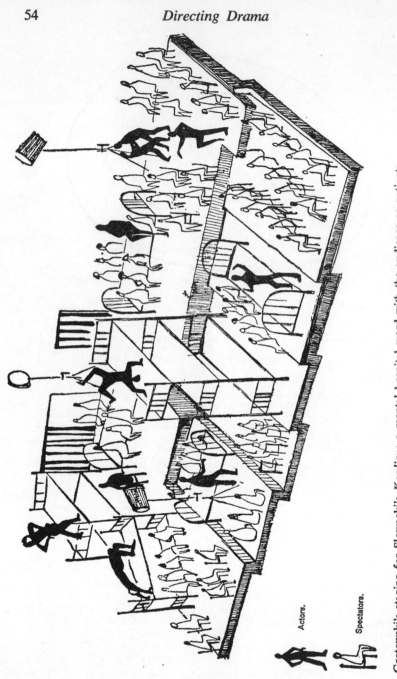

Grotowski's staging for Slowacki's *Kordian*: a mental hospital ward with the audience as patients.

6 *The Actor on the Stage*

The acting areas of the proscenium arch stage are as shown below. For speed and convenience in marking scripts the names of the areas are abbreviated thus: DC = down centre, UR = up right, DLC = down left centre, UL = up left, and so on.

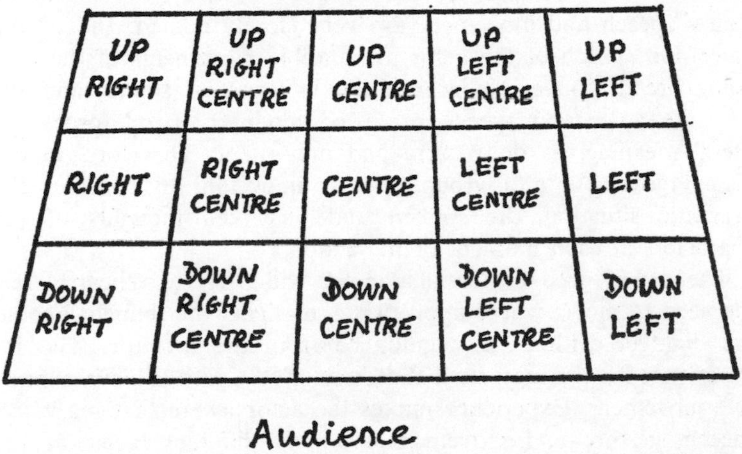

UP RIGHT	UP RIGHT CENTRE	UP CENTRE	UP LEFT CENTRE	UP LEFT
RIGHT	RIGHT CENTRE	CENTRE	LEFT CENTRE	LEFT
DOWN RIGHT	DOWN RIGHT CENTRE	DOWN CENTRE	DOWN LEFT CENTRE	DOWN LEFT

Audience

Figure 1

Note that left and right are from the actor's point of view. 'Upstage' denotes away from the audience. 'Downstage' denotes nearer the audience. The directions 'upstage' and 'downstage' are dictated by raked stages, which slope up from and down to the audience. The directions 'above' and 'below' indicate that something or somebody is upstage or downstage of a certain point; e.g. 'He is standing above the table,' or, 'The chair is below the fireplace.'

55

The directions 'on-stage' and 'off-stage' are related to stage centre; e.g. 'Move that bench on-stage another foot,' or, 'Take the lamp off-stage with you when you exit.' 'In' and 'out' usually refer to flying scenery. Scenery is 'flown in' from the flies down on to the stage and 'flown out' up into the flies out of sight of the audience.

MOVEMENT AND THE ACTOR

Planning the movement and grouping of the actors on the stage requires considerable care and deliberation for it should clarify your interpretation of the play, reflect the thinking of the individual characters and give the audience the stimulus of movement and grouping that holds attention and 'points'* the situation.

Movement on the stage can communicate attitudes, relationships and moods as clearly as the actor's speech conveys specific ideas. Voice, speech and movement are very closely related. Indeed the voice and speech of the actor are audible movements of the outgoing breath conveying information in terms of sound, and the way the voice and speech are used modifies or reinforces the literal meaning, as do gesture and movement. Therefore, in devising movement and grouping it is important to consider the dramatic situation, the spoken and unspoken thoughts of the characters at each moment of the action.

The experienced professional actor will early in rehearsal feel the need to move, where appropriate, to signal the thought behind the dialogue without any guidance from the director. The inexperienced actor may need the director's help to achieve expressive movement. Experience makes the actor aware that his voice, speech, gesture and movement are only different facets of the total process of communication, so that a gesture, look or slight move can, on occasions, be as eloquent as dialogue.

On the stage all movement attracts the attention of the audience – just as dialogue does. If, for example, there are two characters A and B standing still on opposite sides of a proscenium arch stage engaged in dialogue, you will see the eyes of the audience rove back and forth from speaker to speaker like spectators at a tennis match. If, however, A makes a noticeable move during B's speech A will take attention away from B. If it is the intention of the

* See p. 74.

author that this should happen, all right, but if not the audience may miss an important piece of information.

All movement and grouping should have a purpose, which may arise either from the situation or the characterization. Occasionally, however, the director has to reposition a character and there is no obvious reason why that character should move. In a case like this an unobtrusive move can be devised, if it is motivated by a thought in the actor's mind in keeping with the characterization. For instance, the actor may slowly move towards a desk to look at a letter, or pour himself a drink, or feel that he wants to sit in a certain chair. It will appear natural and unobtrusive if the right thought prompts the movement. Movement must be arranged to allow the audience to concentrate on the important points which you, as director, wish them to observe, whether these points are made by speech, individual action or grouping. All gesture and movement start from stillness in the same way that the sound of voice emerges from silence – even if that stillness and silence last only for a fraction of a second. Complete stillness and silence in a flux of movement and sound can raise the dramatic interest to great intensity for a few moments, after which it wanes and it is very rarely that a dramatic pause can be held for more than five to ten seconds without weakening the audience's concentration. Non-stop movement can be as tedious as complete stillness. Movement is governed by the changing stage situation. Movement for the sake of movement can be very distracting and weakens concentration on the salient dramatic points.

Usually at each moment of dramatic interest one particular character should have the attention of the audience, because of something he says or does. Your job as director is to make it easy for the audience to be aware of what is going on. You must contrive movement and grouping so that the audience is looking where you want it to look at the vital moment. You deliberately focus and refocus the attention of the audience from character to character as the situation changes. An experienced cast who have worked together regularly will instinctively strive to do this. You may either block out basic moves with entrances, exits and other main movements and then refine or change these in rehearsal, or, as some directors prefer, allow the movement and grouping to develop by experiment and discussion with the cast. The success of this second method depends very much on the type of play, the experience of cast, the time available for rehearsal and the working methods of the director concerned.

If, as many directors do, you tentatively block out major movement, you have the responsibility of making sure that all moves arise from the dramatic situations and characterizations and that the actors who have to carry them out understand the reason for the moves and can make the movement a manifestation of their own thinking. If an actor is unhappy about a given move get him to try out his own alternative and see if it works.

There follow some general principles to which there will be, of course, exceptions. Even with the scripts still in hands, moves and groupings that you may have painstakingly devised are sometimes surpassed by the group inventiveness of the actors. Try to utilize this if you can. Even if you are not going to pre-block moves for the cast it is wise to have a possible range of moves or groupings in mind as a possible point from which to work in rehearsal.

The audience usually directs its attention to the character on whom the rest of the cast are concentrating. This gaining of attention can be aided by the positioning of the cast within the three-dimensional space of the acting area. Consider Figure 1a, which represents two actors on a conventional proscenium arch stage.

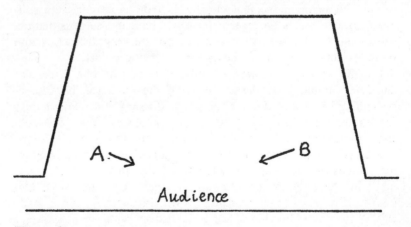

Figure 1a

Actor A is down right and is level with Actor B who is down left. They are presenting the audience with roughly the same proportion of facial and postural communication – so if they are not made-up or costumed to make one more dominating than the other, dramatic interest should be equally divided between them. If, however, Actor B moves to centre stage and looks down right to Actor A, who turns to look at him, the position will be as in Figure 1b.

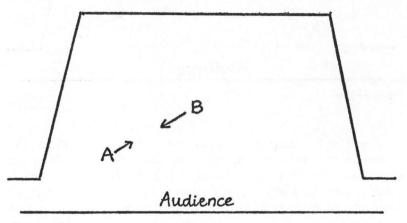

Figure 1b

In this situation Actor A will have weakened his contact with the audience, as he is now facing Actor B and many of the audience will not be able to receive facial or eye reactions from him. Actor B, however, can be seen easily by all the audience. Further, as he has moved to centre stage he should attract more attention, as it is usually an area of dominance.

What has happened in Figure 1b is known as *upstaging*. Actor A is upstaged (has his dramatic position weakened) by being forced to turn away from the audience to act with Actor B, who is upstage of him and is visually more dominant. Grouping and movement patterns must always point the changing centres of interest. Subconsciously the eyes of the audience tend to seek the apex of triangles in the stage image. In Figure 2a Actors A and B have been joined by Actor C. If Actors A and C are respectively down right and down left and both are looking at Actor B, Actor B

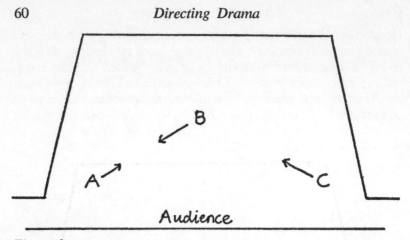

Figure 2a

will still be dominant by virtue of being centre stage, holding the attention of both Actors A and C and also being the apex of the triangle. If, however, when Actor C entered down left Actors A and B turned to give Actor C their full attention the focus of attention would move away from Actor B to Actor C, as in Figure 2b.

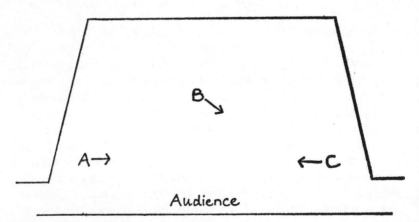

Figure 2b

With Actor D entering up right, as is shown in Figure 3a,

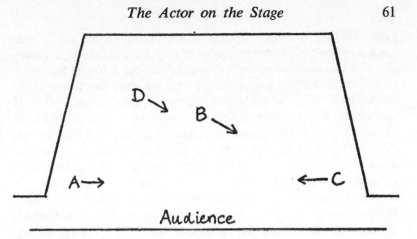

Figure 3a

the focus of attention can still be maintained on Actor C if the entrance is not too obtrusive and Actor D also concentrates on what Actor C is saying and doing. If, however, Actor D makes an entry that commands attention and Actors A, B and C all turn to look at him to hear what he says the new focal point will be Actor D up right, as in Figure 3b.

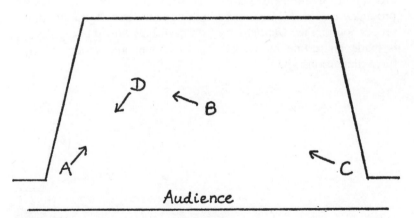

Figure 3b

Here, as in Figure 2a, the dominant actor is upstage and the apex of the triangle. The experienced actor will usually automatically facilitate the shift of attention to a new focal point with some appropriate movement, even if only by a glance that guides the attention of the audience. When rehearsing a naturalistic play with a small cast on a proscenium arch stage the movement often shapes itself with the aid of the dialogue and the arrangement of the setting. The director can accept those moves that accord with the interpretation and appear natural and reject those that do not. With a large cast, or a play that depends for its success on stylization, exactitude or co-ordination of movement, the director will probably have to plan movement very carefully and expect this to be modified during rehearsals. With a large cast there is often the problem of 'masking' where a character upstage is hidden by a character downstage. In rehearsals you have to keep a very vigilant eye on this and check by trying out various seating positions in the auditorium. If masking occurs during a performance sometimes an upstage character can clear it by an unobtrusive movement.

The variety of movement within the acting area necessary to maintain interest and point situations is aided by contrasts in elevation. Characters can stand, sit, kneel, lie on the ground, or use the various levels of the setting, such as rostra, steps, ramps or balconies. In planning movement it is necessary to visualize everything three-dimensionally. The photographs of Peter Brook's production of *A Midsummer Night's Dream* and Robin Phillips's production of *Two Gentlemen of Verona* show how the stage image is made interesting by visualizing movement and grouping on a three-dimensional basis.

7 Notes on the Actor's Technique

Although this book is concerned with the work of the director, it is essential for him to have a knowledge of the actor's technique. Many directors have been actors and acknowledge the value of the experience, as it gave them an insight into the actor's mental and physical processes in creating a character and also a common working language.

The actor is his own instrument – he uses himself: his mental faculties, especially his powers of memory and creative imagination, and his entire physique. These factors are controlled by a disciplined approach to his work, so that a process of creative thinking allows a responsive physique, voice and speech to embody a dramatic character.

For the highly gifted few, acting is an instinctual process in which a vivid imagination triggers a flexible body and a naturally good voice to create a fully fledged dramatic character and an analysis of the technical means by which they achieve this could be daunting and perhaps inhibit the natural free flow of imagination. Normally, an actor acquires his technique through training and the experience of performance, but it should be made clear that there is no single 'correct' approach to the creation of a character, any more than there is any one way of directing a play. The working methods of actors, like those of directors, are necessarily individual and will also vary from play to play, but the thinking behind the approach may be influenced to a greater or lesser extent by the work of Stanislavski or other theorists and by productions and performances that have left memorable images. Stanislavski is still the strongest influence on actor training methods. However, in the translations of his books, *An Actor Prepares, Building a Character* and *Creating a Role*, there is sometimes an expansiveness and circumlocution that could make some aspects of his system lack clarity for the beginner. Therefore, perhaps, it might be wiser for the student actor, under the guidance of a drama tutor, to familiarize himself with Stanislavski's theories through the more concise studies listed in the bibliography and later apply himself to Stanislavski's own works at leisure, remembering that Stanislavski himself said in *Building a Character*:

> This system is a companion along the way to creative achievement, but is not a goal in itself. You cannot act the 'system': you can work on it at home, but when you step out on to the stage cast it aside, there only nature is your guide. The 'system' is a reference book, not a philosophy. Where philosophy begins the system ends.
>
> Reckless use of the 'system', work that is done according to it, but without sustained concentration, will only drive you away from the goal you seek to reach. This is bad and can be overdone, unfortunately this is often the case.
>
> A too emphatic, exaggerated care in the handling of our psycho-technique can be alarming, inhibiting, can lead to an over critical attitude, or result in a technique used for its own sake.

The actor is one of the elements the director uses in shaping his production. With his technique the actor attempts to give an interpretation consistent with the director's overall view. We therefore have the director's interpretation of the play subjected to yet a further interpretation by the actor, who because he is working through the inevitable limitations of his own technique, cannot embody exactly the director's original vision of the staged play. A degree of compromise is built into every production situation.

RELAXATION

Relaxation is, perhaps, the fundamental requirement for the actor. By relaxation is meant the absence of mental and physical tensions that prevent the free flow of the imagination, expressive use of the body and full use of voice and speech. The stresses of normal everyday life build mental and physical tensions of which the

1 and 2 The Mercury Theatre, Colchester. Above: open staging with partial thrust; below: end stage with wings and curtain.

3   The Playhouse, Nottingham. The proscenium arch stage with lighting bridge is in the lowered position on the left. The 26-foot revolve can be seen in the centre and the cyclorama lighting bank top right. The partially raised black shutter shows paint frame room beyond. The fly gallery, with lines, is to be seen on the far side. The house tabs, separating the stage from the auditorium, hang behind the lighting bridge on the left.

4   The Festival Theatre, Chichester. Thrust stage.

average person is unaware. The actor should be so trained that as soon as he becomes aware of tensions he can relax himself by means of simple exercises. Even though the acting situation contains its own special pressures, it is nevertheless of vital importance for the actor that he can be relaxed on the stage, even when he is acting a character under stress. Lack of relaxation shows itself in poor posture, awkward movement, hard or inflexible vocal tones and, of course, self-consciousness. Some directors, if time allows it, start rehearsals with relaxation, limbering, voice exercises and games to loosen up the cast and encourage the feeling of being an ensemble. Being relaxed and at ease gives the actor his essential confidence and also the quality of repose, which enables him to be an essential part of the stage image when not dramatically active, by listening and thinking in character. The director can also, by the right approach, instil confidence in his cast as surely as he can dispel it with the wrong one.

VOICE AND SPEECH

The actor's voice and speech are one of the most important aspects of his technique, for no matter how strongly the actor may have conceived his characterization the ideas the character expresses must be projected to all parts of the auditorium. The projection of voice and speech does not simply mean creation of volume of sound, but using what we call 'forward diction' or 'thinking out' to share the ideas with the audience. On the stage an actor may speak fairly quietly and yet be heard distinctly in the auditorium, if he is relaxed, breathing correctly, has clear articulation and uses 'forward diction'. An audience can be irritated if it misses chunks of dialogue because of sloppy use of voice and speech. On the other hand, an over-conscious use of voice, or over-articulation, is also irritating, if it is not a foible of the character.

The voice has to be balanced with the articulation. A very rich over-resonant voice can drown the articulation, so that we can be very aware of the boom of an actor's voice, but not the words that convey the ideas. Variety in the use of voice is essential if the actor is to keep the audience alert and concentrating. Monotony of volume, pace and pitch of voice are not to be tolerated, as

C

they quickly lead to boredom. One sometimes hears a cast echoing one another's tones, this indicates a loss of concentration on characterization and should be checked at once. It is on the amateur stage that deficiencies of voice and speech are more frequently observed, but it occurs in the professional actor, often as a manifestation of tiredness to which the voice reacts by lack of variety and projection.

PHYSICAL FITNESS

It is essential for the actor to keep himself physically fit, as his ability to characterize and to be flexible in movement and voice depends very much on his state of health. Most actors have a private limbering and voice routine on which they work regularly. Apart from fight scenes or fencing routines that have to be re-hearsed meticulously, the style of production today often requires the actor to use himself in an athletic or even acrobatic manner. A fit and well-exercised body is also conducive to physical ex-pressiveness, so that movement, gesture and facial reactions may effortlessly reflect the thought of a character. As mentioned in the section on Relaxation, five or ten minutes spent on exercises help to impart a feeling of zest and to keep a cast on the *qui vive*.

IMAGINATION

The quality and strength of the actor's imagination is possibly his chief asset. Without imagination he cannot begin to characterize. Each actor normally has his own method of arousing his imagin-ation and applying it to the stage situation. It is the director's job to create the working atmosphere in which the actor's imagination can flower. By a process of encouragement, suggestion, 'feeding' of ideas and images, the director can help the actor to body forth the character or guide the development where this diverges from the agreed interpretation of the play. The director will learn by experience how to handle the different members of his cast. Most actors value the guidance of the director, but some function best if left alone to work things out for themselves, or until such time as they may wish to approach the director for advice. Knowing when to offer constructive comment on an actor's work and when to defer comment until the actor seems ready to take it is an instinct that the director usually develops over a period of years.

EMPATHY

This is the power of the actor to project his character and emotions to the audience and, of course, to give his fellow actors something to react to. It is an outflow of feeling from a character that is sensed and does not necessarily rely on movement or voice. It would appear to be dependent on relaxation, quality of imagination, concentration and confidence. Although almost impossible to describe, one is aware of its presence or absence. Its effect is not unlike a form of radiation that seems to illuminate some actors. It is a quality very evident in actors of the stature of, for example, Olivier, Gielgud, Peggy Ashcroft, Ralph Richardson, Donald Pleasence, Helen Mirren and Glenda Jackson.

TIMING

Timing is the variation of pace, the speed with which cues are picked up, the use of pauses, the silences and stillness in performance that help to feed the content of the play to the audience. Timing also assists clarity, builds and sustains moods and keeps the play moving at the correct tempo to hold the interest of the audience. It is a skill that is polished over years of performance. In rehearsal the director can be of great help to the actor as he times and shapes the performance. One of the qualities of a good production is the exactitude with which dialogue and movement have been timed to shape each moment of the play to give the audience the opportunity to savour every point of dramatic interest. In a poor production the dialogue and action may drag or sometimes rattle on, perhaps at quite a lively pace, but without the variations, changing emphasis, pauses and momentary silences that transform a stream of dialogue into a stimulating flux of ideas and images. The members of the audience need time to absorb the information a play gives them, whether it's conveyed by dialogue or movement, and one way of doing this is by means of a pause. The inexperienced actor often feels that he is keeping up the tempo by maintaining a swift flow of dialogue without the slightest pause, but the pause is the means by which ideas are clarified. It gives time for the audience to digest information. This is one method of what we call 'pointing'. A word can be 'pointed' by pausing before or after it. The brief pause will make the audience perk up and the following word will have an intensified impact. If the actor pauses both before and after the word the 'pointing' will be even stronger. When you are working on a script preparing it for production it is useful to mark the significant pauses. A convenient way of doing this is to make one vertical line for a very short pause, two lines for a longer pause and so on, as follows:

/, //, ///

The pause is also necessary to allow the audience to observe the reactions of the other members of the cast to the dialogue spoken. The pause may be very brief indeed, but the momentary break in the flow of dialogue will enable the audience to observe subtle reactions that are often more eloquent than words.

In the following passage from *Hedda Gabler* Ejlert Lövborg has returned to Tesman's house after a drunken night during which he has lost the only copy of the manuscript containing his finest work. Unknown to Lövborg, Hedda's husband Tesman has found the manuscript and Hedda has hidden it. In this scene Lövborg is alone with Hedda. Following is one way in which the timing could be indicated:

HEDDA: And what are you going to do, then?

LÖVBORG: Nothing./Only make an end of the whole business. The sooner the better.

HEDDA // [*a step nearer*]: Ejlert Lövborg,/listen to me. Could you not see to it – that it is done/beautifully?

LÖVBORG: /Beautifully? [*Smiling.*] With vineleaves in the hair, as you used to imagine once upon a time –

HEDDA: Ah, not vineleaves. I don't believe in that any more. But/beautifully, nevertheless. For once./Goodbye./You must go now, and not come here again.

LÖVBORG: /Goodbye, Madam. Remember me to Jörgen

Tesman. [*About to go.*]

HEDDA: /Wait a minute. You shall have a souvenir/to take with you. [*She goes to the writing-table and opens the drawer and the pistol-case. She comes back to Lövborg again with one of the pistols.*]

LÖVBORG [*looking at her*]: // Is *that* the souvenir?

HEDDA [*nodding slowly*]: / Do you recognize it? It was aimed at you once.

LÖVBORG: You should have used it then.

HEDDA: There it is. Use it yourself now.

LÖVBORG//[*putting the pistol in his breast pocket*]: Thanks.

HEDDA: And beautifully, Ejlert Lövborg. Promise me that.

LÖVBORG: /Goodbye, Hedda Gabler. [*He goes out by the hall door.*]

[*Hedda listens a moment at the door. Then she goes across to the writing-table and takes out the manuscript in its package. She glances inside the wrapper, pulls some of the sheets half out and looks at them. Then she goes across and sits down in the easy-chair by the stove with the packet in her lap. After a moment, she opens the stove-door and then the packet.*]

HEDDA [*throwing some of the leaves into the fire and whispering to herself*]: Now I am burning your child,/Thea. You with your curly hair. [*Throwing a few more leaves into the stove.*] Your child/and Ejlert Lövborg's./[*Throwing in the rest.*] I'm burning it –//burning your child.

End of Act III

Apart from the pauses shown, variations of pace within a phrase or line will help to feed the information to the audience and keep the dramatic intensity at the desired level. The movement within this scene, where nothing is said, has to be as carefully timed as the dialogue. For instance, when Hedda goes to the writing-table, the manner and pace at which she moves must be timed to build the tension, which is heightened when we see she is going to give him a pistol. Lövborg's pause before he says, 'Is that the souvenir?' compounds it. After Hedda says, 'Use it yourself now,' if Lövborg does not savour, in a pause, his being ordered to commit suicide before putting the pistol in his breast pocket and before he replies,

'Thanks', the moment will lose force. Similarly Lövborg's exit must be timed exactly to allow the image to register. If he is too fast or too slow the mood will not hold. Again when Lövborg has gone and Hedda is alone on the stage, her movement as she goes to the bookcase and returns to the stove with the manuscript must be timed to reveal her mental state.

From Lövborg's exit to the end of the act there are only four lines of dialogue, but Hedda's business of getting the manuscript must be timed so that the enormity of her action is fully relished and the fact that she has only four lines to verbalize what she is doing must not be allowed to make this scene too abrupt for its dramatic importance. The timing of business must reflect in the rhythm of the movement the thought behind the action.

TIMING LAUGHS

Laugh lines in comedy and farce have to be put across with exactly the right timing and pointing to galvanize the audience into laughter. The basic technique is:

a. To get the full attention of the audience with the first part of the line.

b. Pause very briefly before the key word or phrase, to build up anticipation.

c. Put it across crisply and clearly to trigger the laugh.

d. Freeze while the audience laughs.

e. Kill the laughter before it weakens, by continuing the action.

In comedy and farce teamwork must be very slick and all the actors must be aware of potential laugh lines so that they don't kill them by speaking or moving when the audience has just started to laugh. All the cast must 'wait for laughs' and try to anticipate at which places they must freeze on other actor's laugh lines. Often it is the reaction of a character to a line that triggers the laugh and without the reaction to the line being seen it loses its force.

In the following extract from *She Stoops to Conquer*, by Oliver Goldsmith, the illiterate Tony Lumpkin hands his mother a letter to read for him, which unfortunately reveals the very secret that must be kept from her.

TONY : But I tell you, miss, it's of all the consequence in the

world. I would not lose the rest of it for a guinea. Here,
mother, do you make it out. Of no consequence! [*Giving Mrs
Hardcastle the letter.*]

MRS HARDCASTLE: How's this? [*Reads.*] 'Dear 'Squire, I'm
now waiting for Miss Neville, with a post-chaise and pair,
at the bottom of the garden, but I find my horses yet unable
to perform the journey. I expect you'll assist us with a pair of
fresh horses, as you promised. Dispatch is necessary, as the
hag, (ay, the hag) your mother, will otherwise suspect us!
Yours, Hastings.' Grant me patience. I shall run distracted!
My rage chokes me.

Amusement will probably build up in the audience to the moment when she pauses before the word 'hag'. If she pauses again
after 'hag', in that pause the amusement should burst into open
laughter and should be boosted if her facial reaction points 'hag'.
In this extract from Act I of Joe Orton's black farce *Loot*,
Fay, a homicidal nurse, is talking to McLeavy whose wife she has
discreetly murdered, after getting her to make a will in her
favour. The comedy arises from the sense of propriety with which
outrageous statements are made. In this extract there are at least
ten possible laughs, which are indicated with asterisks.

FAY: Your wife changed her will shortly before she died. She
left all her money to me.
MCLEAVY: What! [*Almost fainting.*] Is it legal?
FAY: Perfectly.
MCLEAVY: She must have been drunk. What about me and the
boy?
FAY: I'm surprised at you taking this attitude. Have you no
sense of decency?*
MCLEAVY: Oh, it's God's judgement on me for marrying a
Protestant.* How much has she left you?
FAY: Nineteen thousand pounds including her bonds and jewels.
MCLEAVY: Her jewels as well?
FAY: Except her diamond ring. It's too large and unfashion-
able for a woman to wear. She's left that to Harold.
MCLEAVY: Employing you has cost me a fortune. You must
be the most expensive nurse in history.

FAY: You don't imagine I want the money for myself, do you?

MCLEAVY: Yes.*

FAY: That's unworthy of you. I'm most embarrassed by Mrs McLeavy's generosity.

MCLEAVY: You'll destroy the will?

FAY: I wish I could.

MCLEAVY: Why can't you?

FAY: It's a legal document.* I could be sued.

MCLEAVY: By whom?

FAY: The beneficiary.

MCLEAVY: That's you.* You'd never sue yourself.

FAY: I might. If I was pushed too far. We must find some way of conveying the money into your bank account.

MCLEAVY: Couldn't you just give it to me?

FAY: Think of the scandal.

MCLEAVY: What do you suggest then?

FAY: We must have a joint bank account.

MCLEAVY: Wouldn't that cause an even bigger scandal?

FAY: Not if we were married.

MCLEAVY: Married? But then you would have my money as well as Mrs McLeavy's.*

FAY: That's one way of looking at it.

MCLEAVY: No, I'm too old. My health wouldn't stand up to a young wife.*

FAY: I'm a qualified nurse.*

MCLEAVY: You'd have to give up your career.

FAY: I'd do it for you.

MCLEAVY: I can give you nothing in return.

FAY: I ask for nothing. I'm a woman. Only half the human race can say that without fear of contradiction.* [*She kisses him.*] Go ahead. Ask me to marry you. I've no intention of refusing.* On your knees. I'm a great believer in traditional positions.*

MCLEAVY: The pains in my legs.

FAY: Exercise is good for them.*

[MCLEAVY *kneels.*]

Use any form of proposal you like. Try to avoid abstract nouns.*

If you attempt to squeeze the maximum laughter from each possible laugh you may slow the performance and 'milk' it too much, therefore you have to decide which you will treat as moments of silent amusement and which you will treat as major laughs. This is called 'storing laughs'.

Towards the end of the extract the laughs tend to bunch up. This is where you should be selective. This can be contrived simply by not pausing before and after the ones you wish to play down, but give the full treatment to those you select.

In the following extract from Act III of Molière's *The Imaginary Invalid*, the quack Purgon is terrifying the gullible hypochondriac Argan with a list of the dreadful things that will happen to him for refusing to take his expensive remedies.

As Purgon swiftly piles disaster on disaster and Argan quails with each imaginary affliction the comic effect will build until Purgon's last speech.

PURGON: I declare that I abandon you to your evil constitution, to the disorder of your bowels, the corruption of your blood, the bitterness of your own gall and the feculence of your humours.

ARGAN: Oh Lord!

PURGON: I foretell that in four days you'll be in an incurable condition.

ARGAN: Oh mercy!

PURGON: You'll fall into a state of bradypepsia.

ARGAN: Mr Purgon!

PURGON: From bradypepsia into dyspepsia.

ARGAN: Mr Purgon!

PURGON: From dyspepsia into apepsia.

ARGAN: Mr Purgon!

PURGON: From apepsia into diarrhoea and lientery.

ARGAN: Mr Purgon!

PURGON: From lientery into dysentery.

ARGAN: Mr Purgon!

PURGON: From dysentery into dropsy.

ARGAN: Mr Purgon!

PURGON: And from dropsy to autopsy* that your own folly will have brought you to.

[*Purgon exits.*]

If 'autopsy' is pointed as the ultimate of all the grisly horrors, with a pause before it as a 'get ready to laugh' warning and a pause after it for the audience to relish Argan's reaction of terror it will trigger the 'stored' laughter into one big laugh. Purgon can then kill the laughter before it wanes when he continues, '. . . that your own folly will have brought you to,' and make a splendid exit in high dudgeon.

POINTING

Pointing is the technique the actor uses to clarify or emphasize an idea, word or action for the audience. There are various ways in which it can be achieved. As we have seen when considering timing, pausing before or after, or before and after the salient word, phrase, sentence or action makes it stand out.

The actor can also point by making a word, phrase or sentence stand out from its context by changing the volume with which it is spoken, making it louder or softer; by using a different vocal tone; or even by using a different pace, pitch or inflection. Pointing demands a subtle and flexible use of voice and speech.

An action can be pointed by ensuring that the attention of the audience is momentarily directed at that action. This is achieved by having momentary stillness everywhere else on the stage, so that the slightest movement catches the eye of the audience; the image is made to impinge by virtue of its isolation.

An example of pointing an action would be in Act II of *Hedda Gabler,* where Lövborg (who has forsworn drink) takes one of the glasses of punch and says, 'Your health Thea!' to Mrs Elvsted. If Lövborg were to speak as he reached for the glass the gesture would not convey the full significance of his reaction to his belief of Mrs Elvsted's lack of faith in him. However, if all on stage, including Judge Brack and Tesman in the small room up stage, are still and silent for those seconds, Lövborg's action of taking the glass in his hand before he speaks can be a very powerful moment.

CHARACTERIZATION

Every actor has a different approach to the job of creating a character. Some actors like to find their own way into the character and need to have the liberty to experiment without feeling that the director is doing too much of the thinking for them. Others are much more open to suggestion and some ask for positive direction. You must be sensitive to the way in which it is necessary to handle the individual members of your cast. Too firm a style of direction with an actor brimming with ideas may inhibit his creative spark. The comparative freedom you may give to a well-cast and polished actor may leave the actor, who needs the constant guidance of the director, floundering. As director you have to monitor the development of every character; in some cases you will need to do it with subtlety, in others you may be very explicit.

From early rehearsals, by discussion and information the director gives, the cast should be aware of the following:

1. What the play is about. (Theme, message, ruling idea or super-objective.)
2. The plot of the play, with its sequence of events, climaxes and individual involvement in the action.
3. The style or convention of the play. (Comedy, tragedy, farce, fantasy, romance, thriller, play of ideas or a mixture of various styles.)
4. The proposed treatment of the dialogue.
5. The stage settings, furnishings and essential properties.
6. The leading character, what makes him tick and his relationships with the other characters.
7. The other characters in the play and their motivations and inter-relationships.
8. Their own character's physical appearance, attitudes and relationships and, of course, the background of their character so it can be developed in depth.
9. The mood or atmosphere of the play and what creates this.
10. Any relevant details that will help them to visualize their characters, such as: period in history, architecture, costume, music, or social, political or literary background.

In rehearsal the actor may try out various ways of creating his character, such as Stanislavski's advice to think and react 'as if' he were this character in this situation, allowing the dialogue and the physical situations to trigger his reactions and using recollected emotions to fuel the character's emotions, or he may use the stimulus of impressions gathered from any literary or art form, or indeed simply rely on the power of his own imagination and common sense to create a credible character.

The furniture, setting, properties and costumes can, in themselves, be a powerful stimulus to the actor. These external tangible items can, on occasion, fire the imagination and foster that essential quality of truth in the dramatic situation. For instance, a certain chair, walking stick, hat or picture may prove to be the talisman that leads the actor to the full realization of his character. The development of his character will inevitably be influenced by the reactions of the other members of the cast and the guidance of the director. In the early stages of rehearsal he will probably be ultra-sensitive to criticism, although he may not show it, and therefore need very considerate handling by the director. He will also be influenced by the setting within which he is working, the properties he uses, costume, make-up, lighting, music and effects.

Rehearsals are a time for experiment for the actor in which he will gradually, from rehearsal to rehearsal, as the production gains momentum, transform from an actor holding a script to a fully-fledged character. The director will need to assist him with patience and an understanding of the actor's psychology. During rehearsals a rapport often develops between actor and director, so that without words being used the director can guide and encourage the actor by the quality of his attention and sense of appreciation.

8 *Preparing the Production*

THE DIRECTOR AND HIS DESIGNER

The director and his designer usually have a series of discussions at a very early stage of the production to decide how the play will be presented. Sometimes a director is his own designer. Normally, however, the planning of the setting with its décor is a matter of collaboration in which all aspects of the play are discussed prior to the designer making drawings and models of the setting for approval or modifications.

The director needs to have a ground plan of the setting agreed as soon as possible, so he can be certain it will allow the cast to express the play in movement and grouping. It is imperative to be strictly practical and understand what will work in terms of theatre and what will inhibit movement or distract from the content of the play by drawing attention to itself as a piece of scenery. On occasions there is applause for a beautiful set as the curtain rises. This will no doubt gratify the designer, but it may detract from the main fare of the occasion which is the action of the play. Settings should not be too obtrusive, unless, of course, one is aiming for spectacle, but should be a stimulating working environment for the actor. Sometimes an originally splendid idea can 'grow' and obstruct the acting area, cramping movement; like a recent production of *The Cherry Orchard* in which the orchard itself was so thoroughly represented that the settings in which the actors performed were unnaturally cramped and this affected the movement of the entire cast.

There seems to be a feeling these days in favour of simplicity of design, although, naturally, some plays demand elaborate settings for their interpretation. Settings should normally reflect the period, mood and convention of the play, although in recent years there have been many brilliant productions which have made older plays more significant to contemporary audiences by a completely fresh approach to the décor and costuming. Notable examples are the Royal Shakespeare Company's productions of *The Man of Mode* directed by Terry Hands and designed by Timothy O'Brien, and *A Midsummer Night's Dream* directed by Peter Brook and designed by Sally Jacobs.

In the early meetings with the designer there may also be pre-liminary discussions on lighting, costume, projected scenery, effects and pyrotechnics – such as the use of smoke boxes, flash boxes and maroons for explosions. Pyrotechnics require stringent safety precautions and space within the stage area for their deployment.

From the start the cost of the production must be kept in mind in case the design plans become too expensive. The production manager is normally the person who supervises the costing of set construction and he must be consulted to advise on the practica-bility of what is proposed and whether it is within the budget for the production.

When the design of the setting has been approved the designer gives working drawings to the master carpenter or construction crew so work may start as quickly as possible. The designer, if not actually designing the costumes, will want to be consulted about those that are hired or taken from the wardrobe. Similarly the designer will be interested in the lighting of the play, because both the setting and costumes will be influenced by the type of lighting used.

WORKING ON THE SCRIPT

The early stages of preparation involve a study of the script to clarify your approach to the whole production. You must satisfy yourself that you have a thorough understanding of the following: the theme, the style (convention), the plot with the dramatic climaxes, the characters, the language, the subtext, the period, the sound, music and effects required and, of course, the essential re-quirements of the setting, which you are discussing with the de-signer. It is also wise to familiarize yourself with the dramatist's background, his preoccupations, and his other plays.

As you read the play visualize it in action. The series of mental images you receive should give you ideas as to how you can stage it. Try to see the play from the point of view of each character. Put yourself in the shoes of each of them, in the situations in which they find themselves. Remember each character is the centre of his own world, with aspirations, virtues and failings.

In this phase of work you will probably be making notes on all the above-mentioned aspects of the production as well as diagrams and sketches of possible movement and grouping. Don't allow your director's text of the play to become too cluttered with a multiplicity of notes. You can if you wish keep notes on themes, characters, situations, subtext, etc., in a separate notebook, cross-referenced with your director's copy, and keep the latter free for diagrams, sketches, sound, light, effects, curtains and scene change notes, which are the physical happenings in a production. Careful preparation of your director's text will help to make your re-hearsals efficient and progressive. It is the working blueprint for your production.

Some directors note every minute detail of what they want to happen on stage; others do not block any moves or groupings before rehearsals and allow the movement of the play to sort itself out in rehearsal as a result of discussion and experiment with the actors. Coming to rehearsal with no blocking in mind demands plenty of rehearsal time and absolute confidence that you can sort out the movement flow with the actors in discussion and experiment fairly smoothly. It also demands a very experienced director and highly professional cast.

What many directors do is to arrange a tentative blocking of the scenes they are rehearsing, but are prepared to alter or abandon it if it doesn't work and devise something better on the spot. If you do block out basic moves it helps to visualize what you feel are the most effective groupings at the climaxes of the play and plan moves that make it easy for the characters to find themselves in that position at the desired moment. If you start planning moves without knowing where all the characters should be at a certain point you may have to scrap those moves if you find you have put actors in the wrong position, and go back to a point where you can manoeuvre them into the correct strategic placing for the important moment.

When blocking in your copy of the text you must visualize what your moves will look like from all parts of the theatre and check that characters do not mask one another and that all members of the audience will be able to see into the stage picture. It is advisable to use pencil when making sketches or indicating moves, as there are bound to be many alterations made in rehearsals. Blocking for arena and thrust staging calls for particular care and the director has to arrange movement to give the audience a fair share of the viewing, especially of the leading characters.

If you do pre-block moves it is vital to arrange every move in accordance with the thinking of the character. You have, as it were, to get inside the skulls of the characters and to plan moves accordingly. In a particular situation a particular character would probably want to sit, stand, cross the stage or rise to express in movement what he is thinking. In blocking you mentally become each character and act out the scene in your head. Some directors like to use a model of the stage with small figures to represent the actors so that they can get a three-dimensional impression. If your thinking really probes the mind of the character the moves you devise may be excellent, but remember that you, the director, are not the actor you have cast. He is the person who has to make the moves, therefore suggest to your cast that the moves are something to try out, to be modified by them or completely changed if unacceptable. With this approach most actors manage to make given moves their own. However, if an actor says firmly that a move feels very awkward and it is throwing him, invite him to devise his own move and see if it fits into the shape of the scene.

Some play texts include the moves of the original production. These are the work of another director and cast and were also devised within a different setting; they may be quite unsuitable. It is far better to plan fresh moves and business based upon your interpretation of the play. In preparing the production, however, one has to guard against indulging in what the critics will tell you are extravagant gimmicks. Innovations must spring from valid interpretations of the text, as was the case with Peter Brook's highly praised production of *A Midsummer Night's Dream* with its circus stilts, trapezes and juggling.

The period of preparation will be one of fairly intensive work and may occupy several weeks (or months in some cases). This is the time when you will, on your own, apart from conferences with the designer, steep yourself in the text until you feel that you have a firm grasp of the play, an understanding of its inner life, and know how you will arrive at your interpretation.

Many directors prepare their copy of the text by interleaving each printed page of text with a blank sheet of paper on which diagrams and notes may be made. These are usually cross-referenced by numbers, starting at number one for each page. A handy way of arranging this is to get an A4-sized ring file and remove the sheets of the text from the binding, leaving enough unprinted paper to allow holes to be punched for inserting the sheets into the ring file. The blank sheets of A4 paper are inserted between each sheet of text and may be divided into two columns with a vertical line: a narrow column on the outside of the page for notes for the stage management on curtains, lighting, music and effects, and a broad column on the inside of the sheet for diagrams of movement or groupings and notes describing each move (this is shown in the blocking examples). Some directors include their detailed notes on the interpretation of the play on this sheet. If you do this it may clarify things if you make a third column so that stage management instructions, movement information and notes on interpretation are all kept separate. You must find the best arrangement for your own methods of work. Quite a few directors, it is fair to state, do not pre-block in any way and let the movement and grouping evolve in rehearsal, although naturally they have made notes and have a fund of ideas.

The examples of blocking, for a proscenium arch stage production of *Hedda Gabler*, an in-the-round production of *The Rules of the Game* and an open-air thrust stage production of *The Jew of Malta*, show one way of preparing the director's working copy of the play. Also included is a list of symbols commonly used to denote stage furniture and abbreviations of stage positions.

CASTING

The success of a production is heavily dependent upon the quality of the cast. It pays to take time and care to assemble a cast that have not only the necessary temperamental and physical attributes – quality of voice, speech, movement, stage presence and dramatic imagination – for their individual roles, but can balance and work agreeably with the rest of the cast.

For most actors auditions are a nerve-racking business and

Common Symbols for Settings

Small chair

Armchair

Sofa

Tables

Telephone

Fireplace (stage right)

Windows

Open archway

Doors (opening on or off-stage)

Lamp

Rostrum with steps

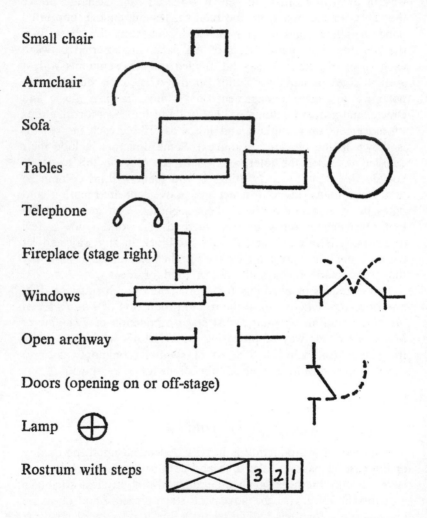

Abbreviations used in Blocking

Cross	X
Cross left	XL
Up right	UR
Right	R
Down right	DR
Up centre	UC
Centre	C
Down centre	DC
Up left	UL
Left	L
Down left	DL
Up right centre	URC
Right centre	RC
Down right centre	DRC
Up left centre	ULC
Left centre	LC
Down left centre	DLC

The directions are from the actor's point of view as he stands on the stage. Left is the actor's left.

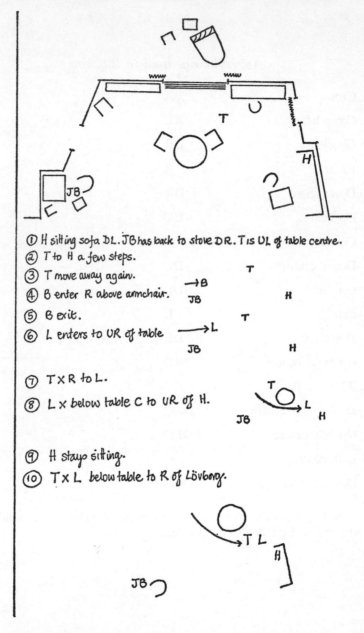

① H sitting sofa DL. JB has back to stove DR. T is UL of table centre.
② T to H a few steps.
③ T move away again.
④ B enter R above armchair.
⑤ B exit.
⑥ L enters to UR of table
⑦ T X R to L.
⑧ L x below table C to UR of H.
⑨ H stays sitting.
⑩ T x L below table to R of Lövborg.

BRACK: ① What do you mean by 'the worst'?

HEDDA: If he won't go with you and my husband.

TESMAN [*looking at her dubiously*]: ② But, Hedda dear, do you think that would quite do, for him to stay here with you? Eh? Remember Aunt Julle can't come.

HEDDA: No, but Mrs Elvsted's coming. So the three of us will have tea together.

TESMAN: ③ Oh, that will be all right, then.

BRACK [*smiling*]: And perhaps that might be the wisest plan for him too.

HEDDA: Why?

BRACK: Good gracious, my dear lady, you've often enough said hard things about my little bachelor parties. They weren't suitable for any but men of the strongest principles.

HEDDA: But surely Mr Lövborg is a man of strong enough principles now? A converted sinner –

④ [*Berte appears at the hall door.*]

BERTE: There's a gentleman, ma'am, who'd like to see you.

HEDDA: Yes, show him in. ⑤

TESMAN [*quietly*]: I'm sure it's he. Just fancy!

⑥ [*Ejlert Lövborg comes in from the hall. . . . He remains standing by the door and bows abruptly. He seems a little embarrassed.*]

⑦ TESMAN [*crossing to him and shaking his hand*]: Well, my dear Ejlert, so at last we meet once more!

LÖVBORG [*speaking with lowered voice*]: Thank you for your letter, Jorgen ⑧ [*Approaching Hedda.*] May I shake hands with you too, Mrs Tesman?

⑨ HEDDA [*taking his hand*]: I'm glad to see you, Mr Lövborg. [*With a gesture.*] I don't know whether you two –

LÖVBORG [*with a slight bow*]: Mr Brack, I think.

BRACK [*returning it*]: Of course we do. Some years ago –

⑩ TESMAN [*to Lövborg, with his hands on his shoulders*]: And now you're to make yourself absolutely at home, Ejlert. Mustn't he, Hedda? For you're going to settle down in town again, I hear. Eh?

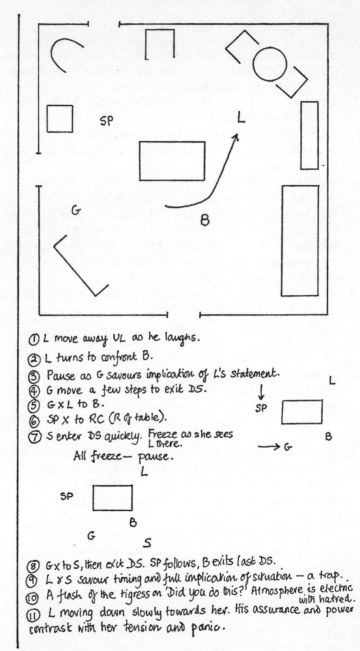

① L move away UL as he laughs.
② L turns to confront B.
③ Pause as G savours implication of L's statement.
④ G move a few steps to exit DS.
⑤ G x L to B.
⑥ SP X to RC (R of table).
⑦ S enter DS quickly. Freeze as she sees L there.
       All freeze— pause.

⑧ G x to S, then exit DS. SP follows, B exits last DS.
⑨ L & S savour timing and full implication of situation — a trap.
⑩ A flash of the tigress on 'Did you do this?' Atmosphere is electric with hatred.
⑪ L moving down slowly towards her. His assurance and power contrast with her tension and panic.

LEONE: – No, no, my dear Venanzi! Not mine: your own!

GUIDO: Very well then: mine! But *you* will be dishonoured!

BARELLI: Disgraced! We shall be forced to expose your dishonour!

① [LEONE *laughs loudly.*]

BARELLI: How can you laugh? You'll be dishonoured, dishonoured!

LEONE:② I understand, my friends, and I can still laugh. Don't you see how and where I live? Why should I worry my head about honour?③//

GUIDO: ④ Don't let's waste any more time. Let's go.

BARELLI: But are you really going to fight this duel?

GUIDO: Yes, I am. Don't you understand?

BARELLI: No, I don't!

LEONE: Yes, it really is his business, you know, Barelli!

BARELLI: You're being cynical!

LEONE: No, Barelli, I'm being rational! When one has emptied oneself of every passion and . . .

GUIDO ⑤ [*interrupting and gripping* BARELLI *by the arm*]:   Come, Barelli. It's no use arguing now. Come down with me, too, Doctor.

SPIGA: ⑥ I'm coming! I'm coming!

⑦ [*At this moment* SILIA *enters. There is a short silence during which she stands still, perplexed and amazed.*]

⑧GUIDO [*coming forward, very pale, and grasping her hand*]:   Goodbye, Silia. [*He turns to* LEONE.] Goodbye.

[GUIDO *rushes out, followed by* BARELLI *and* SPIGA.]

SILIA: Why did he say goodbye like that?

LEONE: I told you, dear, that it was quite useless for you to come here. But you were determined to.

SILIA: But . . . but what are you doing here?

LEONE: Don't you know? I live here!

SILIA: And what is Guido doing? Isn't . . . isn't the duel going to take place?

LEONE:⑨ Oh, it will take place I suppose. It may be taking place now!

SILIA: But . . . how can it be? If you're still here?

LEONE: Oh, yes, I am here. But he has gone. Didn't you see him?

SILIA: But then . . . that means . . . Oh God! Why has he gone? Has he gone to fight for you?

LEONE: Not for me, dear – for you!

SILIA: For me? Oh, God! Did you do this⑩

⑪LEONE [*coming up to her with the commanding, disdainful air of a cruel judge*]:   Did I do this? You have the impertinence to suggest that I am responsible for it!

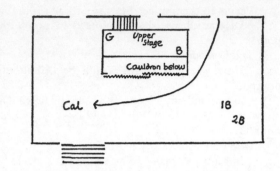

① G offer gold.

② G to UR of upper stage.

③ Cal and 1 Basso and 2 Basso enter UL. Cal to RC.

④ B to C of upper stage — above cauldron.

⑤ G hold up knife. (On trumpet cut cable.)

⑥ On trumpet 1 Of and 2 Of fast entry (UL & UR) to open curtains.

⑥ Quick sequence
a - trumpet
b - cable cut
c - B into cauldron
d - explosions
e - light cauldron
f - Officers open curtains
g - cauldron thrust forward

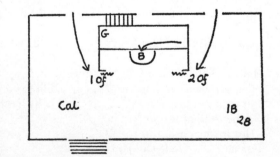

GOVERNOR: Oh excellent!① Here, hold thee, Barabas!
I trust thy word, take what I promised thee.

BARABAS: No, Governor, I'll satisfy thee first:
Thou shalt not live in doubt of anything.
Stand close,② for here they come. Why is not this — to audience
A kingly kind of trade to purchase towns
By treachery, and sell 'em by deceit?
Now tell me, worldlings, underneath the sun
If greater falsehood ever has been done.③

[*Enter* CALYMATH *and* BASSOES.]

CALYMATH: Come, my companion bassoes, see I pray
How busy Barabas is there above
To entertain us in his gallery;
Let us salute him. Save thee, Barabas!

BARABAS: ④ Welcome, great Calymath.
Will't please thee, mighty Selim-Calymath,
To ascend our homely stairs?

CALYMATH: Ay, Barabas;
Come, bassoes, attend.

GOVERNOR: Stay, Calymath;
For I will show thee greater courtesy
Than Barabas would have afforded thee.⑤

KNIGHT [*within*]: Sound a charge there! ⑥

[*A charge, the cable cut, a cauldron discovered into which* BARABAS *falls.*]

although an actor's technique may enable him to appear relaxed in most circumstances it is possible that under audition conditions the actor may do himself less than justice. It is therefore up to you as director to ensure, as far as you can, that actors are put at ease and do not feel that they are caught up in a rushed, impersonal process where they have only a brief time to display their talents. The mass auditions held by some managements are typical of this and are an off-putting experience for a sensitive player. Amateur companies usually have a more considerate approach.

If possible, let the people auditioning have a copy of the script in time for them to read the play and decide on an initial approach to the part for which they are auditioning. Ideally they should be aware of the style, the nature of the language, the period and their own role in the context of the play as a whole. On occasions a fluent and lively reader at an audition cannot develop a fully rounded and projected character in rehearsal, because movement and physical attributes don't match up with the impression given by the use of voice and speech. If possible, therefore, include one or two improvisations and also several audition pieces that the actor feels represents his best work.

Type-casting – that is using actors who are very similar in temperament and physique to their stage roles – is still fairly common in both the professional and to some degree the amateur theatre. This is something that many actors resist – unless they feel that steady work in the same type of part is better than long periods of unemployment. It is also sometimes the penalty of excelling in particular 'type' roles. The late Sonia Dresdel often found herself playing dominant and ruthless women because she was brilliant at it and it was rarely that she was offered parts where her true warm nature could be revealed.

It occasionally happens that you make a mistake in casting; the actor belies the impression made at audition and during rehearsals it becomes clear that a change must be made. This is a painful decision to have to make and there are bound to be strong feelings generated, but your duty is to the success of the production. You must also consider the rest of the cast, because one character who is not correct can upset the balance of the whole production. It is essential to make any cast change as soon as possible.

Casting in small established companies is often limited to members of that company, but it has the advantage that the talents and potential of everyone will be known and there is an opportunity to give actors the chance of broadening their range. Also in the small established company it is possible to create very good working relationships, which are not so easily achieved in an *ad hoc* situation.

Don't attempt to direct and act at the same time, unless you have the calibre of a Gielgud, because the points of view are, as it were, 180 degrees out of phase. The director is out in the auditorium tuning the performances of all the cast and gauging the possible reactions of an audience from all parts of the auditorium, while the actor's main concern is the development of his character within the stage situation and projecting this to the audience. It is unusual for one person to fulfil both functions satisfactorily.

THE PRODUCTION CONFERENCE

When the production has been planned and the setting and the physical arrangements for the production have been decided, it is necessary to have a meeting of the production team, where everyone will have an initial briefing about the production and be given details of setting, décor, rehearsals, lighting, costumes, furniture, properties, sound effects, music and a look at the set model. This meeting puts everyone in the picture and subsequently the production manager will see people individually and co-ordinate the work of the team and check that all items will be ready on the dates required.

A Progress Check is a useful way of ensuring that everything goes smoothly, that nothing is overlooked and that deadlines are observed. This check can be enlarged or cut according to the scale of the production. You will see that most of the items concern the work of the production team and business management, but as director of the whole operation you may want to ensure that everything is on schedule and all is going smoothly. Efficiency helps to give the cast a feeling of confidence, while last-minute delays and panics are demoralizing.

Progress Check

PRODUCTION   REHEARSALS START   FIRST PERFORMANCE

---

1. Costing ....by:
2. Scripts available ....by:
3. Set design completed ....by:
4. Production Conference ....by:
5. Casting completed ....by:
6. Rehearsal Call Sheets ....by:
7. Furniture/Props ordered ....by:
8. Posters ordered ....by:
9. Programmes ordered ....by:
10. Tickets ordered ....by:
11. Handbills ordered ....by:
12. Preliminary publicity ....by:
13. Costumes ordered ....by:
14. Wigs ordered ....by:
15. Licences: play/taping ....by:
16. Advertising in ....by:
17. Furniture/Props ready ....by:
18. Posters/Handbills ready ....by:
19. Tickets ready ....by:
20. Set completed ....by:
21. Costumes/Wigs received ....by:
22. Sound ready ....by:
23. Lighting ready ....by:
24. Photo call ....by:
25. Programmes received ....by:

THE REHEARSAL CALL SHEET

In consultation with your production manager and stage manager
you will need to prepare a Rehearsal Call Sheet that gives full
information about the place, day, date, time, scenes to be rehearsed, costume parades, photo calls, dress rehearsals and open-

ing performance. This gives everyone, cast and production team, a clear view of the work in hand and the time available. Of course, between the commencement of rehearsals and the opening performance there will be the inevitable alterations that the stage manager passes on to all concerned.

SCENE AND CAST ANALYSIS

With a large cast, especially if there is to be a lot of doubling of parts, it is often useful to make a scene and cast analysis. This also shows the rehearsal units into which the play has been divided. Many classical plays and some modern ones (for example, those of Brecht) are often written in fairly short scenes which are often units of convenient rehearsal length. For a full-length play not written in short scenes you will find that each act can be broken down into rehearsal situations. Most plays can be divided into approximately twelve to thirty situations for concentrated work in rehearsal. An example of a scene and cast analysis is shown for a production of Marlowe's *The Jew of Malta.* An analysis like this allows you to call only those members of the cast needed for the scenes you are rehearsing. It can be very frustrating for actors to hang about, sometimes for hours, waiting to rehearse.

The number of hours available for rehearsal will govern the quality of the production. There is no hard and fast rule about rehearsal time. It depends very much upon the play, the cast and the working methods of the director. In the professional theatre from two weeks in a regional repertory company to twelve weeks in a major theatre company, working a five- or six-hour rehearsal day, seems to represent the range. In the amateur theatre rehearsals at evenings and weekends can be spread over a longer period of time than the average professional production, but in most amateur companies an intensity of rehearsal is called for to acquire and polish techniques that the professional has as a tool of his trade. When working with amateur casts you have to gauge how much rehearsal they can beneficially take. The director of an amateur company will often find himself in the role of drama tutor as well as director, which will absorb some of the available time.

CAST ANALYSIS FOR THE JEW OF MALTA BY CHRISTOPHER MARLOWE

Cast Required

Page	Scene	Rehearsal Unit	Situation	Machevill	Barabas	1st Merchant	2nd Merchant	1st Jew	2nd Jew	3rd Jew	Governor	2 Knights	2 Officers	Calymath	2 Bassoes	Abigail	Friar Jacomo	Friar Bernardine	Abbess	Nun	Mathias	Lodowick	Del Bosco	Ithamore	3 Slaves	Katherine	Bellamira	Pilia-Borza	4 Citizens
9	Prologue	1	All guiet. Prologue. Profile by guile and grace.	✓	✓																									
11	I·i·A	1	B reveals wealth. Turks arrive. G takes		✓			✓	✓	✓																				
18	I·ii·A		Turks demand tribute. Jaws money		✓						✓	✓	✓	✓	✓															
26	I·ii·B	2	A becomes nun to find B's cache.		✓											✓					✓	✓								
33	II·i		A finds cache.		✓											✓														
36	II·ii	2	D-B brings slaves. Counters Turks. Slaves bought.		✓						✓	✓				✓							✓							
38	II·iii·A		Slaves to rights. False challenge.										✓								✓	✓		✓	✓	✓			
45	II·iii·B	3	B sends false challenge.		✓						✓		✓			✓					✓	✓		✓					
54	III·i	3	P-B gives Bell. silver. I desires Bell.																					✓		✓	✓	
55	III·ii		M's L. Kill each other.										✓								✓	✓						
57	III·iii		I tells A of murder. I enters convent.													✓	✓							✓				
61	III·iv	4	B and I poison porridge.		✓											✓	✓							✓				
65	III·v	4	G refuses to pay Turks.								✓	✓		✓	✓								✓					
67	III·vi		Nuns dead. A tells Friars.													✓	✓	✓										
69	IV·i	5	Friars try to blackmail B. Are killed.		✓												✓	✓						✓				
78	IV·ii		P-B and Bell. con I to rob B.																					✓		✓	✓	
84	IV·iii	5	P-B extracts more money.		✓																			✓		✓	✓	
86	IV·iv		B disguised. Poison'd flower.		✓																			✓		✓	✓	
90	V·i		B betrayed. B helps Cal.		✓						✓	✓	✓											✓		✓	✓ (as Turks)	
95	V·ii		G prisoner. B now Governor.		✓						✓	✓	✓	✓	✓								✓	✓		✓	✓ (as Turks)	
99	V·iii	6	Mess. invites Cal. to feast.										✓	✓	✓													
100	V·iv		G prepares to defect to Turks.								✓	✓											✓				(as mess)	
101	V·v		G traps B in cauldron. Cal. is prisoner		✓						✓	✓	✓	✓	✓								✓				(as citz)	✓

9 Rehearsals

'The director is a one-man audience through whom
I prepare for a real audience. He is the focal point
at which, during rehearsal, I aim my performance.'
PAUL SCOFIELD

Before rehearsals commence your planning should be completed. During rehearsals the various members of the production team, apart from those assisting at rehearsals, should be occupied ensuring that the set, furniture, properties, costumes, lighting, sound effects and music are ready on or before the date required.

Rehearsals may be on the stage where the production will be presented, or in a hall or rehearsal studio. Substitute furniture and properties – usually anything suitable the stage management can lay their hands on, will be used for some weeks and the acting area, entrances, stairs, windows or other features, will be marked on the stage with chalk or adhesive tape to give the actors the feel of the proportions and disposition of the setting. This work should be completed before the cast arrives so that no time is wasted. Punctuality is of prime importance. The first rehearsal is important because you can set the tone of the working atmosphere, make introductions, start welding the disparate members of the cast into an ensemble, subtly instil enthusiasm and make the company aware of your confidence in the play and casting.

Most directors commence proceedings by talking about the play and the way in which it is proposed to stage it. At this first rehearsal the designer is usually present with ground plans and a model of the set. Everyone gets a chance to inspect these and see how they have been represented for rehearsal purposes by odd tables, chairs and markings on the floor. There may be some preliminary discussion about costumes, properties, furniture, light-

ing, effects, music and other things that will receive more attention
in later rehearsals.

The next step is usually a reading of the script to mark cuts and
alterations, to begin to sort out the ideas and relationships and
to settle queries. In this first reading the actors are getting used to
the voices and personalities of the rest of the cast, the language of
the play and its dramatic situations. It is usually a good idea for
everyone to read quietly to pick out the sense of the dialogue and
not to attempt to characterize at this stage. A few directors do
not give their actors a script at first, but use the cast as a group to
explore the situations in the play by means of improvisation. When
the dramatic situations are clarified in this way, they then turn
to the script. Of the vast majority who start from the script, most
have only one or possibly two readings and then start moving the
play, but there are those like Roger Planchon of the Théâtre
National Populaire at Villeurbanne who like to do extended work
on the text itself. In his rehearsals for *Gilles de Rais,* Planchon
had the cast reading the play round a table for three weeks, during
which time the set was built; only then did the cast start to move
the play inside the actual set. This is an extreme example and most
actors would get restive if not under the spell of a director of the
calibre of a Planchon. You may have to spend more time on readings if the text is a complex one or if the language and style of
dialogue demand detailed attention and you feel it is better to
tackle this in readings than when you have the play moving.
Sometimes a director reverts to a few readings to work on certain
aspects when the play has been fully blocked.

When you are ready to start moving the play, if you have
already blocked out major moves in your director's copy of the
text, it is a good idea to phrase your directions to the actors in
such a way that the cast understand you regard your blocking
as tentative and if after trying your given moves several times the
actors are still uncomfortable, then you want them to say so
and you and the actor concerned will devise something better.
So you might, when giving your pre-planned moves, phrase your
instructions, 'I thought you could come downstage on that line,'
or, 'Try crossing right after she sits down.' This sounds more
open than a directive. If you are autocratic about pre-planned
blocking the actors may feel constrained and perhaps have some
difficulty in approaching their roles with free-ranging imagination.

5   The Phoenix Theatre, Leicester. Open stage.

6   The Crucible Theatre, Sheffield. Thrust stage.

7 The Royal Exchange Theatre, Manchester. Theatre in-the-round.

8 The Victoria Theatre, Stoke-on-Trent. An in-the-round production of *Circus Adventure*, a play for children by John Ambrose Brown.

You are more likely to obtain performances of depth from your cast if you work as a team and devise an environment in which discussion, experiment and encouragement lead the actor to characterize from a body of inner truth and understanding that has surfaced in rehearsals, than if you adopt a dictatorial attitude. The usual practice is to block the basic movement of each situation or unit and then for the cast to walk it through to see if it feels right, while the director checks if there is masking, or if any move or grouping looks unsatisfactory on the stage.

If you firmly establish the style of the production during the time when you are rehearsing the first units it will set the tone for the rest of the play and you should find that the concentrated work on early rehearsals makes subsequent rehearsals go smoothly. If you are working on a play in which the women wear long skirts, arrange for rehearsal skirts to be worn. It will help movement and sense of character.

During rehearsals the stage manager, or assistant stage manager, who is acting as prompter, will be noting moves in the prompt book. This is the working copy of the text which will contain every practical detail of the production including cues for lighting, sound, music, effects, and fly gallery. It will be used by the stage manager to run the show from the prompt corner. There are a few points worth mentioning here. Some companies do not use a prompter if the stage manager runs the play from a control room at the rear of the auditorium. This makes the actors responsible for getting themselves out of a 'dry'. With productions on a thrust stage, or in-the-round, the prompter frequently sits in the front row. In very small or amateur companies the director's copy can serve as a prompt copy if it contains all necessary information.

If you are working on a three-act play, for example, it is necessary, as rehearsals proceed and you start rehearsing scenes in, say, Act II, to go back and spend a rehearsal on Act I to keep it fresh. In the same way, when working on Act III you will periodically have to run Acts I and II to keep them going and to build continuity. When you and the cast are happy with the basic movement of a rehearsal unit you can then start concentrating on the finer points of production. It is advisable to have a clear aim for each rehearsal. Each situation in the play will have its own theme or objective, relevant to the main theme or super-objective of the play. Bear this in mind as you work in detail on scenes

D

dealing with the characters and character relationships, dramatic climaxes, timing (pace, pauses, silences, stillness), variety (pace again, volume, pitch, voice), pointing, audibility, teamwork and development of business.

During early rehearsals, if you are rehearsing in a theatre, you may be on the stage with the actors or in the front seats, so that you are in close contact with the cast, to discuss aspects of the production as they arise and devise the basic blocking. When the blocking is completed and the whole play is moving, it is advisable to reposition yourself further away from the stage so that you can check that what is happening on the stage is registering at a distance. You will have to monitor audibility (some theatres have 'dead' spots) and also view the pattern of movement and grouping. It is wise to vary your position and try out the extreme left and right stall seats and also to sit as far back as you can get and as high as you can at the back of the circle or balcony. If you have been working in a rehearsal room you will have to check these points as soon as you can after you get on to the stage, because the intimacy of the rehearsal room has probably toned down the scale of the playing, which may need to be adjusted for the theatre.

During rehearsals the lighting designer should watch the play through, be given a ground plan with the main areas of action indicated, be briefed about the setting, hear the director's views on lighting requirements, special effects, the time, season and the atmosphere of the locale and of course the colour of costumes and settings. He should have discussions with the designer and the more thoroughly he is briefed the more efficiently he will be able to light the play.

BUSINESS

'Business' is the small movement personal to a character that is developed during rehearsal. It is unwise to attempt to impose business on an actor as it arises from his characterization and situation. You may have visualized a comic routine that an actor can carry out with some property, which seems to you quite brilliant, but the actor has to make it work. Therefore, feed the general idea to the actor and if he thinks it's a good one let him work on it himself so that the carrying out of the idea is his own creation. In rehearsal, of course, you can comment on and polish his business.

Some play texts have the business of the original production printed as well as the basic movement. Consider very carefully before you use any of this and make sure it agrees with your production and the characterization. The best thing is to let the actor invent his own business, but you will have to view it with your directorial eye to ensure that it is in key with the production and that he has not elaborated it out of proportion. Business can give an added dimension to a production and imprint memorable images. For instance, in Lindsay Kemp's production of Oscar Wilde's *Salome,* Salome's ecstasy when she had been given the head of John the Baptist was portrayed in a brilliant bit of business when the severed head emerged from a slit in the side of the skirt of Salome's shimmering costume. This was contrived by an actor being inside the voluminous skirt. The image was unforgettable and in a moment conveyed more information than any words could have done.

IMPROVISATION

Improvisation is an invaluable tool in training the actor. It can also be used in rehearsal to aid the development of character and to give a fuller appreciation of situations that in their scripted forms have not fully stimulated the imaginations of the cast, so that they can return to the script with fresh insights and an understanding of the implications behind the dialogue.

If, for example, the actor and actress playing Lövborg and Hedda in Ibsen's *Hedda Gabler* were having difficulty with the scene quoted earlier, where Hedda is persuading Lövborg to commit suicide, setting up a similar situation, where one person is prevailing upon another to similar purpose, but inventing fresh characters and improvising dialogue, could supply the appropriate mental images to help the actor and actress to characterize Ibsen's characters with greater depth.

However, improvisation is a tool to be used with discretion in rehearsals. On occasions a session spent on an improvisation, especially with amateurs, generates valuable insights into situation and character, but it will take time out of your rehearsal schedule and not all actors will find it the best way of using their rehearsal time. Working with the author's script supplies the exact thoughts, language, reactions and situations for that particular play and the subtle director can feed ideas, images and suggestions that will fire the imagination of the actor as surely as improvising a comparable situation. Indeed, working and reworking a scene giving difficulty in an exploratory manner is in itself a form of improvisation.

The director must always strive for spontaneity of thought and action. Although dialogue is printed and movement is planned they must be invested with absolute freshness at every rehearsal and performance. There is always an apparent set-back when scripts are first put aside and fluent rehearsals with scripts in hand are temporarily replaced by an emphasis on remembering the words. This is where the director needs patience to allow the cast to slowly think their way through the scene and take as many prompts as are needed. When fluency is gained your prime task will be to see that the thoughts behind the words are revealed and that the actors don't simply deliver a fluent stream of dialogue. It may take a few rehearsals from the word-perfect stage to reach the point where the ideas behind the dialogue are absolutely clear.

Some directors want words to be learned as soon as possible, but most directors want the characters and the situations developed first, so that the thoughts of characters in the dramatic situation can give the dialogue greater subtlety and depth and the words are acquired from a sense of full dramatic involvement.

The words 'open' and 'closed' are sometimes a useful way of describing the success of an actor in projecting the thoughts of his character in the dramatic situation. The 'open' actor allows us to, as it were, see into his mind, to share his thoughts and feelings. There is no barrier between him and the audience; all is clearly revealed. The 'closed' actor, on the other hand, while possibly very audible and outwardly polished, does not allow the audience to share his thoughts and feelings so easily. The audience have to probe in an attempt to find out what is going on inside him. The director needs to check that an outer gloss does not hide lack of content in performance.

Occasionally, when time is short, there is a temptation to show an actor how to achieve a certain effect. Usually it is better to give him the impression of what is needed by feeding ideas, imagery, similes and metaphors, and allow him to find his own way of expressing it. In this way the final performance will have the authority of the actor behind it. On the other hand there are actors who ask to be shown what you mean and there are also highly successful directors such as Ingmar Bergman and Samuel Beckett (when directing his own plays) who do demonstrate, when an exact piece of timing, intonation or movement is required.

When you have got to the word-perfect stage you can try running scenes as 'stoppers', in which you tell the cast that you are concentrating on certain aspects of production, such as cues, timing, pointing, variety or climaxes and not to be put out by being halted for a quick note, before continuing with no loss of momentum. After a 'stopper' have a 'non-stopper', in which you keep quiet, to restore the flow, and give notes only at the end of the scene.

If for some reason a rehearsal is becoming lifeless you can try what I call a 'shake-up' run, in which the scene is played very fast, very loudly with large gestures and exaggerated movements with the cast doing just what they like. It is relaxing, often great fun and certainly shakes the actors out of a rut. As you can imagine, there are plays with which you would be loath to try such tactics, but as in love and war – so with directing – all is fair if it achieves success.

The director receives the transmission of the actor from the stage, savours what is given and sends back his impressions in much the same way as an audience, for whom he is the substitute in rehearsal. Sensitive actors can feel the quality of your attention and respond to it, although you may say little or nothing. It is, as Reinhardt called it, a psychic evocation of performance from the actor. Be attentive, courteous, decisive and encouraging. Use your sense of humour, the leaven of labour, and try to keep interruptions to the minimum when a scene is going well – give notes at the end.

If one or two members of the cast are experiencing a problem it is better to give them a special half-hour rehearsal on their own, rather than hold up the rest of the cast while you deal with it. Also some comments are better made in private than in front of the whole cast.

Occasionally an actor becomes spiky or argumentative. If this happens let him free-wheel for a short time – say nothing and don't comment on his work. Eventually, slightly anxious, he may approach you for your opinion. Actors don't like to be ignored.

As rehearsals proceed and the production begins to take shape it is wise to check with the production manager that all the jobs under his control are on schedule and all will be ready for technical and dress rehearsals.

As soon as the set is up, view it from all parts of the auditorium, particularly from the extreme left and right seats of the front stalls and the back of the highest circle or balcony to check lines of sight, the set itself and setting of furniture. It will pay to check from all angles even if you are working in-the-round or on a thrust stage. Also invite the cast to try out the set, opening and closing doors, using practical windows, sitting in armchairs and on sofas and generally familiarizing themselves with the working environment. If possible have a dress parade well before the dress rehearsal to give time for any costume alterations. At the technical rehearsal the cast will adjust to the stage management working through a routine, operating music, sound, effects, curtains, lighting and scene changes to see that all function smoothly. Both cast and director will need infinite patience, as hitches inevitably occur, and lighting and sound levels have to be adjusted, scene changes rehearsed and timed, curtain and lighting cues timed, and a multitude of other details attended to.

Some directors like to have a word rehearsal before the play opens. A convenient time is usually when the setting-up is taking place and it is not possible to rehearse on the stage.

In the late rehearsals the actors take over. You feel, to use a metaphor, that the garment you have designed has been woven by the cast with so many personal contributions that it is theirs to display.

DRESS REHEARSALS

The dress rehearsals are another time when patience, tact and humour are needed by all. They are the occasion when every element of the production is conjoined in sequence of performance: music, curtains, sound effects, pyrotechnics, costumes, wigs, scene changes, lighting, make-up and special effects.

As the stage manager will be in charge of the running of the show you will be free to sit well back in the auditorium and take notes. Try sitting in a different place for each act to check visibility and audibility.

If all is on schedule everyone will be saved the irritation of people still sawing, hammering and touching up the décor. It is quite maddening trying to conduct a dress rehearsal with work that should have been completed still audibly in progress. This is why deadlines must be observed. When all is ready an air of efficiency prevails and this gives everyone a feeling of confidence. Last-minute panics are very unsettling to a cast, apart from being a waste of time. If all is well-organized and your first dress rehearsal runs smoothly subsequent dress rehearsals will allow time for the cast to consolidate their performances.

There will, of course, be various stops during your first dress rehearsal. Although you will have given curtain, lighting, sound, music and other timings in the technical rehearsal, there will be adjustments.

Your concentration will be mainly on the technical matters, while the cast will be incorporating all the new factors into their performances. As in the first rehearsals without scripts, there may be a set-back, but do not be dismayed, the new circumstances have only momentarily impaired concentration.

When you stop the action of the dress rehearsal for a necessary re-timing of an entrance, cross, lighting cue or sound effect make your remarks briefly, clearly and cheerfully. Don't allow a minor point to develop into a time-wasting debate. Also check that people have had time to note down what changes you have requested. For a 'dry', ensure that the member of the cast is re-cued so that they get the link-up and not just the prompt. Often for the first dress rehearsal there is no make-up, but the wardrobe people will be in attendance to make any further changes to costumes. In this and other dress rehearsals there are so many items that have to be noted that it is helpful to have a production secretary with you, so you can quietly dictate notes on items for which you are not going to stop the action. If you yourself try to write and watch and listen some fault may pass unobserved. A cassette tape-recorder is a useful substitute.

Three dress rehearsals are recommended. An invited audience for the last dress rehearsal helps the cast to get to grips with audience reaction, especially for the timing of laughs.

The curtain call is an essential part of the performance and should be rehearsed. Audiences need to release their feelings of appreciation in applause and a well-rehearsed curtain call is the professional way of returning the compliment.

10 *Directors at Work*

In this section seven contemporary directors talk about their methods of work. Six are professional directors and one is from the amateur theatre.

I asked each director approximately twenty questions concerning their personal approach to the staging of a play. Not all the questions were phrased in the same way and frequently the answers were extended to include valuable comments on theatre generally.

What emerges clearly is that each director has his own individual attitude and method, and that his approach is different for each production. Also it is clear that the experienced director achieves his best results by creating working conditions in which the actor is given a creative freedom within the bounds of the agreed interpretation for the particular production.

I should like to express my gratitude for the enthusiasm and openness with which all these directors have discussed their working methods – often in the middle or at the end of a busy rehearsal day.

DAVID BUXTON

David Buxton is the Artistic Director of the Mercury Theatre, Colchester, which opened in 1972. He has worked in the theatre for many years and was an actor and stage manager before he became a director.

How long do you like to work on a text before starting rehearsals?

It's difficult to say; usually I've been ruminating on a text for months. This *Reluctant Heroes* thing we decided to do as the opener for a new season as long ago as last November. It's true that when we made the decision it was left a little bit loose, so we could have changed it. When I read it last November I already saw its possibilities as an opener. I tend these days to do quite a bit of intensive work on a play for about a fortnight and then leave it at that and go into rehearsal.

Does a lot of the thinking crystallize in rehearsal with the practicalities in front of you?

To a degree, yes. One has, regrettably, to make certain decisions before the company starts rehearsals, because of practical difficulties with the construction of sets and costumes. Ideally, what I would like is for the company to do a fortnight's work on the play, then for me to talk to the designer, and for the company to talk to the designer as well, and hammer out how we are going to do it and then start a further three-week rehearsal period. This is not economically possible, so I have to make decisions about how something or other is done at least three weeks or so before we go into rehearsal. I find that I get fairly confident about the sort of decisions I make and I very rarely have to change something, but I like things flexible as far as the actors are concerned.

Do you follow any routine in this pre-rehearsal work on the text or does it vary from play to play?

It's very hard to say. In some ways it's easier to do intensive planned work on plays that I don't like very much. Plays I'm very fond of I tend to read. I start at the beginning and think, 'Would this work well if we had two entrances up there, or do we need a third?' And even at the sixth time of reading the play, after about four pages I find that I am caught up with the excitement of reading it. And it's very difficult to sort out how the excitement is in fact working – what is in fact making it exciting. In plays I am ambivalent about, I can do rather more disciplined and scholarly work.

You've got to dig out the way to make it work?

Exactly. One, as it were, makes a list of the problems implicit in the play.

At what stage do you bring in the designer?

We have two designers. And before we went on holiday we dis-cussed in vague shape the three major productions that I am doing this season. I am doing the productions of *Reluctant Heroes*, *The Importance of Being Earnest* and *Hamlet*. I went on holiday on 14th June and came back on the 26th or so, and *Reluctant Heroes* had hardened off very nicely. The designer showed me the designs when I came back. However, we had both gone off the original idea for *The Importance* and we had a brand new plan. She came back with this new scheme a fortnight ago and I was rather wild about it. She then did some sketches and a few days ago she gave me the ground plan and I've taken that away and looked at it. *The Importance* goes into rehearsal just two and a half weeks from now.

Do you collaborate – giving the designer an equal say?

The designer has a pretty equal say. We get our best results if I make detailed notes. About *Hamlet,* one knows the play so well it is surprising to realize how long it is since one has actually read it. During the last three months I have started to read it through on various occasions, but have been distracted by urgent things that have cropped up. So I had to start from the beginning each time.

Do you ever find yourself saying to a designer, 'I want three doors and I want them there, there and there. I want steps, rostra and various levels, this is definitely what I want?' Do you ever dictate what you require?

I tend not to. Naturally with *The Importance* one works out how many entrances there are and the designer sketches very freely in the first instance and I understand the direction it's going to take and I felt that there must be a central entrance for Lady Bracknell in Act I and Act III and the bookcase must go over there, for example. I do insist on some things, such as not wanting this play done in a realistic set. We must find some way of stylizing it. One of the best bits of design we did was for *The Cherry Orchard*. This took a lot of experiment before we found exactly what we wanted.

So you always have a ground plan before rehearsals start?

Yes, and there is a model that we can all look at, otherwise the tradesmen – carpenters, electronics and the wardrobe – are going to be desperately behind.

Working to a schedule you have got to have everything exactly on time.

Very much so, but one always has to allow for some things to be altered, even at a late stage. It's a mug's game trying to keep carpenters waiting.

Do you have your major movements blocked before rehearsals start, or do you like to leave everything open, if you have the time to spare?

There is no spare time to spend, but I find more and more I am leaving things open, because the final result is better. I used to block things rigid. What I do now is to block things roughly and I do this before the ground plan is finally approved, so that I know that if the worst comes to the worst I can refer to notes. What I thought originally was that on this line you walk down there and he moves over there and then you go over there, then we've got people where we want them. Now I find it much better, even in plays I know have to be highly stylized, to try to make the actors find the moves 'right' for them. It's not that one leaves them entirely without suggestion. I am constantly making suggestions, but I encourage the actors to move about themselves.

For general grouping no doubt you would have to use your director's eye and not leave it entirely to the actors?

Oh, yes! One is trying during the blocking, even at a blocking rehearsal, to make some sort of sculptural shape, but if it is clearly not going to seem right to the actor, it's just not going to work, so that one has to compromise.

So large basic moves you might have blocked, whereas minor moves will be left to the actor?

It's difficult to be hard and fast about this. In the set for *Macbeth* we had quite a tall staircase with a gallery and it would be damned silly if, because of what the actor said, we played the dagger scene on the floor and did not use the gallery. One has to make a decision and carry it through. The possibilities of the set must be used.

Apart from your director's copy of the text, in which you have presumably made some drawings and notes, do you have your stage manager or prompter record moves and business?

Yes. I find this very useful. Because neither the actors nor I have infallible memories and if the prompter can say, 'Last time he was down there,' it is a great help. We find that it is invaluable to have a meticulous record of what we had decided at the last rehearsal. Moves that are changed very late may not be in the book. We don't make a fetish of it.

How many hours would you say you manage to put into a production, including the technical and dress rehearsals?

We try to rehearse all the hours there are, within the three weeks. We don't rehearse in performance time. I don't go a bundle on evening rehearsals when the theatre is closed. People get very tired in extra evening rehearsals and you don't get good work out of them and the chances are that you won't get good work out of them on the next day either. We start work in the morning at a quarter past ten and rehearse until one o'clock and then rehearse from two fifteen until five o'clock, except when there is a matinée.

Do you normally give a preliminary talk to the cast at the begin-

*ning of rehearsals about the author, the play, the period, the cos-
tumes, etc.?*

I get self-conscious doing it, but I believe very firmly that it is
a good thing to do. I should say why, because I have thought
about this quite a lot. At the beginning of the rehearsal it is the
director's responsibility to point everybody in the right direction.
Then I like to block it – some people don't like blocking, but I
like to block the play from beginning to end. This takes a couple
of days and as you get the cast piecemeal during blocking, so a
preliminary talk is the only opportunity you have of trying to get
something across to them as to how you want it to be done. When
they are rehearsing with a book in their hands they want to know
where I want them to stand, or where we decide, as I like to put
it these days, and they're not going to be thinking about the play
in general – they're going to be thinking about trees rather than
woods. Then, it seems to me, the director's job is to start something and be somehow the chairman, as it were, of a committee,
and he has to blow the whistle and get it together at the end. The
beginning and the end are terribly important. So I always say a
word or two, sometimes not very much. I feel it is important, on
the sergeant-major principle, when you're doing an army play
for instance, that you can show the troops that you have a very
firm idea how the play can be done.

So you may give an example of the style.

Exactly.

*Would it be fair to say that you have a variety of approaches –
some things you block, while some things are free, you like to
experiment and the approach is pretty democratic?*

I should hope so. I have little opportunity these days of seeing
other directors at work. I trained myself as a director by first
being a stage manager, and I saw an awful lot of directors working. Only someone observing me at work could comment on how
I do it, but I am conscious of approaching different plays in
different ways.

You just said you trained yourself to be a director by working a

*great deal in stage management. Do you feel this is the best way
to learn the fundamentals of directing?*

It's one way. I came into the theatre with ambitions to be a
director. I was an actor, perhaps I wasn't a very good actor, and
as I wanted to be a director I went into stage management. It was
work I liked doing. I liked being on the book. I was a good
prompter and sensitive to the actors and found it fascinating. I
worked with many directors, so I was able to pick their brains,
as it were. When I first started I used to say, 'Don't you think it
would be a good idea if . . .?', but I soon learned to shut up. I
learned a tremendous amount by just watching what people were
doing.

*Many directors I have worked with have tended to be autocratic,
but things seem much more democratic in the theatre now.*

Yes, that's the way that suits me really. I'm not much good at
being an autocrat. I'm a confidence man. A confidence trickster.
I persuade the actor that he can do it. I suppose it's a process of
encouragement. It's not in me to be really rude to a man. I can
on occasions be pretty firm, but I find the new open method of
directing suits me rather better. I've no doubt that the actors in
the pub might characterize me as being rather easy-going in rehearsals, but I don't really mind, it's the results on the stage that
matter.

*How many readings do you like to have before you start moving
the play?*

We usually only manage one, because of the time factor, of course.
Sometimes it's useful to read a play more than once; usually not.
It depends on the play. With *The Importance* one could well read
the play several times during rehearsal. I don't think it would be
much use reading it twice, straight off the reel.

But you might stop moving the play and go back to a few readings?

Yes. I find this useful with authors who write highly stylized plays.
If a play doesn't seem to be coming out in the right style, I might

go back to a complete reading of the text to get at the style and the rhythms.

Do you usually keep moves as they have been blocked out, or do you change things – even up to a late moment of rehearsal?

If necessary, up to the last moment, but certainly not for the sake of it. With moves, sometimes you have to backtrack to a point where you can arrange the grouping more satisfactorily. You might say, 'When you move, don't go down there, go up there and then you can move across here.' I find that one of the things about devising moves is that I often get better results if I work backwards, as it were. I might be rehearsing and then visualize this fabulous grouping, where there is a central character, and there is a 'pull' from this character here and a 'pull' from that character there. Then you have to backtrack to see how you can arrive at this particular grouping that exactly reflects the tensions between the characters. Perhaps, for example, you may want a character to be in the middle and able to look right and left and able to exert the maximum 'pull' – that is a triangular situation. You then work backwards to see how you can get the characters into those positions. I've been doing this instinctively for years, but it's the first time I've actually expounded the idea. With younger directors, I do notice that they are not so conscious as people of my generation where the strong points on the stage are. If you want to get somebody to do something good and strong you've got to not only get them on to a good position on the stage, but you've got to group the other characters to maximum advantage for the situation.

Do you mean they don't have such a strong pictorial sense?

No, not just pictorial, but in the sense of appreciating the forces that are made by sculptural shapes in groupings. I am more interested in forces than in the picture. One can make the picture look pretty quite late by arranging minor details. For me the pentagram of forces on the stage is important, so that you've got strength in the dramatic situation.

At what stage in rehearsals do you expect your actors to be word perfect?

I never ask people to come in next morning word perfect. I like them to learn at their own rate. I employ actors who are not lazy, but if somebody doesn't know it then everybody else suffers. I find that actors vary as to when it's good for them to drop the book. It is important that they can 'give' to the other actors as soon as possible, so that they have something to react to; of course, it's difficult for them to do this when they're still holding the book. If someone still has his nose in the book and time is getting on, I might say, 'You should, by now, be giving something back to your fellow actors, either by eye, face, gesture or body movement.' I believe it's a big mistake to allow actors to go away to study their parts and think, 'Here I have these lines; how can I make them live?' What you've got to do is to get the actor to learn his lines so that he gets a reaction from the other people in the play. It's not what lines mean that is so important, but the reaction they will cause, which is progressive. What lines mean is subjective. It is surprising how quite experienced actors ask how a line should be spoken, when the reaction that is implicit in the reply to that line clearly indicates how the line should be said to get that certain reaction.

How many dress rehearsals do you like to have?

We now open on a Wednesday. We cut Sunday work to the minimum, Monday is a normal working day, no costumes, and normally we have the possibility of two run-throughs in a rehearsal room away from the stage with all the props while the set is being built. On the Tuesday morning, somehow or other, by working overnight and in the morning, by twelve o'clock noon, we should have finished lighting. We then immediately start a technical rehearsal with the cast and all costumes and we do a stopping dress rehearsal. I don't usually cut to cues or entrances, because if you do that you may find you have cut out the moment when you take your coat off and you haven't got a peg to hang it on. Then not later than eight or half-past we start the full dress rehearsal. On the Wednesday, one has on occasions done a word rehearsal, or bits of the play, but usually we have a dress rehearsal at a quarter past two on Wednesday afternoon which finishes at five or half-past, leaving just time for everybody to have a bite to eat before we open.

Helen Mirren, in a letter to the press, stated that she felt that the technical side of theatre – computerized lighting, scene shifting, music and effects, and elaborate costuming – militated against the all-important relationship of the actor with his audience. Do you feel that there is any truth in this?

Yes, it's a trap one can easily fall into if only because the more elaborate the staging is the more time the technical effects take – the technical rehearsals and the dress rehearsals. So in the time when the actor should be warming up and getting ready to face the audience, he is, instead of concentrating on the basic thing of his performance, worried about all the technicalities. It's as simple as that. Obviously it depends on the show, but it's a very easy trap to fall into.

If you can't have three theatres in a complex like the National, although here you do have a main theatre that adapts from proscenium arch to open and a studio theatre, is there any theatre form you particularly favour?

This theatre was built as an open theatre with possibilities of closing it in to a proscenium arch style, if there is a play for which proscenium arch staging is particularly suitable. I much prefer it as an open stage. But it poses problems in certain plays which are easier to do in a proscenium arch theatre. But they are all challenges which are worth overcoming. It works marvellously for two sorts of play. It works marvellously for the epic play like Shakespeare, where you have a group of people who react one to the other and then one of them breaks off and directs the audience to another aspect of the action, or for Brecht, or where music is introduced. It works marvellously where the actors relate strongly to one another, like *The Caretaker* for example, where you have three characters who bring on their own preoccupations and react one to the other. The challenge is when you are doing Wilde, Coward or highly stylized comedies where the actor appears to be playing with the other actors, but in fact has an ear cocked for audience reaction and is consciously aware of the audience all the time. This is true of most high comedy and is true of a farce like *Reluctant Heroes.* This is where the open stage presents a challenge, because it is much easier to do it on a proscenium arch stage, where it is very easy for me, say, as the actor to feed you, and you just turn your head slightly downstage and make some flip remark and all the audience can see you raise your eyebrows. I find it most invigorating to change over from proscenium arch to the open stage, for most of our productions.

RICHARD COTTRELL

Richard Cottrell is the Artistic Director of the Bristol Old Vic Company, which is comprised of three theatres, the Theatre Royal, the Studio and the Little Theatre.

How long, in an organization such as this, do you manage to work on a text before starting rehearsals?

I like to know as long ahead in advance as I possibly can what I am going to do when I am producing a play, because although one may not be consciously thinking about it, and it may sound a little high-flown of course, but you do carry it around with you. For instance, I've known for about nine months that I'm going to be doing *Hamlet* in September. I suppose that for actual reading and work on the text one doesn't get more than four weeks before one starts rehearsing. I generally try to lock myself up for two weeks before I start rehearsals to do some really concentrated work.

Is there any routine you tend to follow in this pre-rehearsal work?

It varies a bit depending on the play, but certainly I tend, with scenes that have more than three or four people, to pre-block them before I start rehearsals. That is a sort of security for me really. It gives me a feeling of security and it gives the actors something to react to and generally saves a great deal of time. If I had a six- or seven-week period of rehearsal I probably wouldn't bother with pre-blocking at all. But in a three- or four-week rehearsal period you've got to get a move on. I generally start, certainly with classical work, with a certain amount of academic reading, which again very frequently isn't awfully helpful, but it gives one something to react to. I try and cut the text as late as possible, if it has to be cut, and I'm a great rewriter and changer of words.

I am interested to hear you say you do some pre-blocking because so many people today say they don't pre-block, but with a tight time schedule one has to do a certain amount.

You have to have plenty of time to be in a position to come to rehearsals without some pre-blocking in mind.

At what stage do you bring in the designer?

As early as I can. Once I have a vague idea – it may only be a single image in my head. Then that's the time to throw it to the designer and get his imagination working.

When you get the designer in, do you, as director, say to him, 'This is what I want and this is my ground plan and I'd like you to execute something on these lines,' or do you say, 'This is an idea and use this as a starting point for your own ideas'?

Mostly the latter. If it's a naturalistic play then I may not. I may stipulate that the table, say, is in the middle, but if it's not a naturalistic play then I leave the designer as free as I can. The designer goes away and gets his imagination working and comes back with his ideas and we talk about those. He'll then go away again and then, depending on the designer, start producing sketches or models and then we'll go through three, four, five or six of those perhaps until we've got it right. So that when we start rehearsals we know precisely what we're up to. The set will be agreed, especially because of the building and painting time schedule. The set has to be agreed and it's got to be costed apart from anything else, at least three weeks before rehearsals start. When the basic set has been arranged, if it's a naturalistic set then one can start putting the furniture into the room.

So you always have a fixed ground plan at the start of rehearsals?

Yes. That's partly of course because of the time element, particularly in an organization like this which once the season has started – we go from the end of August to the end of June – we're producing three plays every four weeks, so it's a bit like a factory. All the departments work to a careful schedule. It has to be very carefully organized and if we have a very big show coming up they'll sometimes start making that particular wardrobe and wigs the production before.

Apart from your director's copy of the text, do you have the stage management record your blocking?

Yes. They record this in the prompt book, yes, because the pre-blocking is something that one alters, throws away, modifies the whole time. It's just my flask of brandy, but the record of what happened at the rehearsal has to be in the stage manager's book.

How many hours of rehearsal do you manage to get in on an ordinary production?

Well, the average play rehearses here for three weeks and is rehearsed for about thirty-three hours a week, not including technical and dress rehearsals. So we get over a hundred hours on the average production. We rehearse from ten in the morning until one and then from two until five on Mondays to Fridays and on Saturday mornings.

When you are starting rehearsals do you give a preliminary talk to the cast about the period, costumes, settings, style, etc.?

Yes, always.

What sort of working atmosphere do you as a director set up for your cast in rehearsal? Do you give them a certain amount of freedom to move as they will and experiment with their characters and relationships, or is time so short that you have to define things rather closely?

No. I give them as much freedom as I can. With somebody who's playing a leading part I would generally discuss the broad lines of the character before rehearsals had started, particularly if you are dealing with somebody who is, say, playing the title role in *Hamlet*. You don't have time to discuss the 'why' in rehearsals – you have to devote rehearsals to 'how'. The 'why' having been decided before.

Do you feel you have a distinctive or very individual approach to directing?

The one thing I do feel, very strongly, is that the well-directed play appears not to have been directed. The best compliment I was ever paid was when somebody once asked one of the critics why – because this person was kind enough to think that I wasn't too hopeless at it – why I didn't have the kind of image that a lot of other directors have. And this critic said that he thought that it was because with my work you never saw the director's hand on the work. You were simply shown the work. That I took as a compliment.

How many readings do you like to have before moving the play?

Generally, only one. We read the play then we get on with it. Sometimes we'll read a scene and we'll discuss it before we start putting it on the floor. Sometimes we won't start with the text at all. Sometimes we'll start by improvising. Improvisation is just a means to an end; it's not an end in itself. It's only useful if you use it to get somewhere.

Do you continually change your basic moves up to a late stage of rehearsals?

One's continually changing.

Right up to the last moment?

Yes.

Gielgud does this doesn't he?

Yes, but I don't drive the actors mad, like Sir John! He drives them into a frenzy by altering things the whole time. One's always modifying the whole time, because one has to try to keep, as Hobbes said, 'working in a steady direction towards an approved end.' At the same time you have to try to look on every rehearsal as a fresh experience. When you come back to rehearsing a scene, you say to yourself, 'Now what am I being shown?' So obviously that will allow for continual modification, because you may not like what you see.

At what stage of rehearsals do you like people to be word perfect?

In the sort of period that we work in, by the last week. It varies slightly, depending on who the actor is. I don't have a lot of hard and fast rules, because every actor is different and has different problems. Every actor has to be treated in a different way.

About improvising – do you use this a great deal to try and reach inner meanings and resolve relationships in a production, or is it only a thing you use occasionally?

It's not something I use invariably. Occasionally, really. I use it if we have a problem. I use it to solve problems.

Do you find that older actors take to this easily or are slightly diffident?

Not really. I find that older actors are sometimes quite brilliant at improvisation.

How many dress rehearsals do you feel are necessary?

Our schedule here, for plays in the Royal Theatre, which is the main house, is that they open on Wednesdays, so we do a technical dress rehearsal, which takes all of the Monday. Then we do three dress rehearsals after that. In the other theatres it's a technical and two dress rehearsals.

What sort of breathing space do you manage to give your casts between the last dress rehearsal and the opening?

I am required by Equity to give them a breathing space of two and a half hours.

If you remember, Helen Mirren wrote to the press some time ago about actors being burdened by the techniques of dramatic presentation?

Yes, I remember that extremely clearly.

She felt that a great deal of over-elaboration, with computerized lighting, scenic techniques, music, sound effects, elaborate costuming, etc. militated against the actor-audience relationship. What do you feel about this?

I think the actor can get swamped by production effects and certainly the relationship between the actor and his audience is the most important thing. I don't like scenery. With the classics I try to keep the stage as empty as I can, but I feel costumes are important.

As a director are there any changes you'd like to see in working conditions in theatre?

Longer rehearsals. Not like the Moscow Art Theatre necessarily, but there is an optimum rehearsal period for a play and that is different for each play. I remember reading in Tyrone Guthrie's autobiography once – he was talking about *Hamlet*. He said, 'If you and your Hamlet really know what you really want to do, the optimum rehearsal period for the tragedy of *Hamlet* is three weeks.' I'm not sure I quite agree with him, but I do see what he means. I think there is a tendency in the theatre for people to talk, rather than do and I'm a great believer in saying to actors, 'Don't tell me, show me.'

If you couldn't have three theatres in a theatre complex, which you have here in Bristol and the National Theatre has, can you suggest a form or even name a theatre that does accommodate itself to most forms of drama?

I personally don't think that the eighteenth-century theatre design has ever been improved on, because it seems to me to give a very good actor-audience relationship.

Is there any particular ideal in the theatre to which you aspire?

I believe very strongly in the permanent company – the ensemble. It's very much a matter of the actors trusting and respecting each other. If they trust and respect each other they will be more pre-pared to take risks and the theatre, it seems to me, is all about taking risks. You have to try to create a working atmosphere in which the actor is prepared to make an absolute fool of himself and not feel that he has failed, because in rehearsal what you often do is fail – often.

I think it was Peter Hall who remarked, 'One has the right to fail.' Do you agree with that?

I think the right to fail is very important, because it is the same kind of thing as the right to take risks. The pressure of having to have a success every time can be intolerable.

Is there any advice you could give a young director wanting to enter the profession?

See a lot of plays. Get to know a lot of actors. The more you know the better. Get a job doing anything, absolutely anything, in the theatre. I think the director is not a sort of *deus ex machina* figure. He is one of the workers in the theatre and therefore the more he knows about every aspect of how the theatre works the better he's likely to be. The other thing, I think I would say, is don't bother what *you* think the play is about, try and discover what the author was intending the play to be about. Our job is to interpret the author.

ALFRED EMMET

Alfred Emmet, O.B.E., is the founder and former Artistic Director of The Questors Theatre, Ealing, London, which is one of the most successful amateur theatre companies in the United Kingdom.

How long do you like to work on a text before starting rehearsals?

This does vary, of course, because it is very much a practical matter. But I would normally hope to work on a text for the minimum of three months.

Do you have any regular routine that you follow on that work on the text – a series of points that you want to resolve?

It varies from play to play. The most important thing I like to do is as much research as I possibly can. My last production was *Three Sisters* and I spent a great deal of time re-researching – because I had done the play before – into the background and various productions of Chekhov's plays and so on. I think research is the most important aspect – the rest depends so much upon the play. Obviously one is trying to probe into it in the greatest possible depth that one can.

Do you work with the designer from the very first opportunity?

Yes.

Do you give the designer a firm outline of your basic require-ments, or is it a collaboration on a fifty-fifty basis, or do you perhaps give your designer a completely free hand?

I think in practice it's a matter of discussion. With some plays one may have a very firm idea of how one wants to direct it, because that may be the reason why one is directing that particular play – but in giving directions to the designer I'm always very careful to give them in very general terms, because the last thing I would want to do would be to block out the possibility of a creative contribution by the designer. So I think the design of the staging evolves as a result of quite a lot of prolonged discussion with the designer.

At your first rehearsal do you normally like to have a firm ground plan and a model, or do you like to keep things flexible for a short time?

Both. I have a ground plan and a model. That is absolutely essential, but everything is kept, to a certain degree, flexible, right up to the last dress rehearsal.

To what extent have you blocked the basic moves before the first rehearsal?

I always block the basic moves before I start rehearsals of any particular scene or act that I'm going to block in rehearsal. I would never come to a first rehearsal in which I'm going to block the moves without having planned it out in detail beforehand, but that doesn't mean to say that that's rigid in any way – one may normally change that quite a lot.

How many hours of rehearsal do you manage to put into the average play, including technical and dress rehearsals?

I suppose one hundred and twenty to one hundred and thirty rehearsal hours. That's what I would say for an average play. In my last production, *Three Sisters,* I was able to get and use about one hundred and seventy rehearsal hours, excluding technical and dress rehearsals, and I found that invaluable. Certainly when I started directing, years ago, I couldn't have made full use of that length of rehearsal time. But I find as I go on I can use more rehearsal hours, that is, make something out of them. On this last production, for instance, I felt that there was not a lot more I could have done even if more time was available, and that was after one hundred and seventy rehearsal hours.

Over what period of time are the one hundred and seventy hours spread?

April 4th to June 19th – about eleven weeks, with a short break for the Easter holiday, but that was exceptional.

Do you usually give a preliminary talk to the cast on the author, the play, period, costumes, mode of staging or do you leave these things to arise in rehearsals?

I think a preliminary talk is important, with discussion as one goes along. I believe it is important for everybody to have at least a general idea about some common aim or direction from the beginning. I find if one talks at great length and in great detail and thinks to oneself, I've covered all that, one deceives oneself very much, because at that stage of rehearsal a great deal of all that information will probably go in one ear and out of the other, because they have not been working on the play enough to assimilate it and take it in, so one has to keep on coming back to quite a number of, even major, points. But I wouldn't like to go into rehearsal without some talk, discussion and preliminary guidance. I certainly think it's important at the first rehearsal to be clear about the mode of staging, the costumes and basic information.

How many readings do you manage to have?

Three Sisters was a special case and in another way too – with enormous success. I tried something I've never tried before and that is I got the cast to read the play very very slowly without any attempt to express it, quite monotonously. This is an idea I've had in my mind for a long time, because I've always been begging actors in early rehearsals, 'For God's sake don't act – I don't want a performance. I want you to discover things.' Then I was very much encouraged when I read in an article that Roger Planchon adopted precisely this method of very, very slow reading over a period of three weeks, before he allowed the actors up on their feet at all. I found this approach immensely valuable. Of course, the cast thought I was quite crazy and it was a mad idea, but after we had done it a bit they found it tremendously valuable. The point being, I think, one has to explore as one reads, and as one listens to other people reading in that way one is really listening to the words with time to understand them, to consider and think about what is behind the words, to get the basic back-ground. I found this very valuable. For many years my basic method of rehearsal has always been to take a section of the play, for example the first act, and to rehearse that intensively for quite a long time before I start any work on the second act. In this instance, first of all I did very slow readings of the whole play then slow readings of the first act and so on. Occasionally, even after we had moved it, we sometimes went back to very slow readings again, which the cast welcomed and found very valuable and then we repeated that process with Act II. So Act I was already learned and working and then we started with the very slow readings of Act II. I found this worked out very very well indeed.

So you set the style that fed into subsequent acts?

Yes. There's a lot you can learn about a play only by a great deal of detailed work and if you establish that at the earlier part of the play it carries through the whole play. Also it means that actors are having to cope with a small section of a play at a time. It's my job as director to see that it is all working into a whole. Of course one has to give it time to get running again, to cohere again, after you have finished with detailed work and start the last fortnight or so of rehearsals. This slow work means that the actors are able to concentrate on studying one single section of the play at a time, and you never have this appalling business of suddenly having to do Act I without books on Monday and Act II without books on Tuesday and Act III without books on Wednesday, which inevitably means an enormous amount of prompting. Working in this way actors are able to arrive at a word-perfect stage without any problems or difficulties at all. This is an enormous help with regard to the progress of rehearsals.

What sort of working atmosphere do you like to create – do you favour a rather disciplined or a free and easy approach?

I think these are two objectionable extremes. I think they must be disciplined. I would think it appalling if any actor were ever late for rehearsal. That sort of discipline is of prime importance. During the rehearsals for *Three Sisters* there was only one occasion when an actor was late and that was when there was a real snarl-up in London traffic. I find that actors accept this sort of discipline without any sort of problem whatever. What I do dislike is discipline in the sense of telling the actors all the time what to do – you do this, you do that, you move here, you move there – in an authoritarian sort of way, because I don't think for a moment that gets the best out of the actors. So, if by 'free and easy' you mean an atmosphere in which the actors are encouraged and helped to be creative and come out with their own ideas and thoughts then free and easy is the way.

Do you find that you tend to change movements or groupings at quite a late stage in rehearsals, or do you regard basic blocking as fixed after a couple of weeks?

I am always prepared to change moves in rehearsals – right up to the last moment, if necessary. I find that if I have really prepared the blocking well, with a subjective feeling from the actors' point of view of what they are being asked to do, I don't often have to change a great deal. But one does come up against scenes which are being difficult and don't work, then very often one will find that a small change in a move or group provides the key that helps the thing to work. This can happen right up to a very late stage. I think it's very important to keep an open mind about that. I would never ask an actor to carry out a move, if I had not, in my own imagination, identified myself with the actor in the character. I imagine myself carrying it out and feeling right.

At what stage of rehearsals do you like the cast to be word perfect? You have, of course, partly answered that one.

Stage by stage. For instance I would probably, for intensive rehearsal purposes, break an act up into three sections. For *Three Sisters* the first act, which I see from the timing took a little under three-quarters of an hour on its first run-through – this I broke into three sections, so that for each section I would spend six to nine hours of rehearsal on a scene that might be expected to play for, say, fifteen minutes and then expect no books for the next rehearsal. This means that by the time you come to rehearsals without books the actors are very familiar indeed with the scene, as it has been worked over in such detail.

How many dress rehearsals do you usually like to have?

We normally have three. The first one is about six days before the opening night.

What sort of breathing space do you give your casts between the last dress rehearsal and the opening?

I like to have the last dress rehearsal the night before. When the actors are still in top gear.

Do you feel that there is a particular type of play that gives you scope to use your individual qualities as a director?

One likes to think of oneself as a director for all kinds of play. I think it is the fact that I have been more successful with the plays of Chekhov and plays of that kind, not that any play is necessarily the same kind as Chekhov. I have of course directed a very wide range of plays, some reasonably successful, some less successful, but I don't know how far the less successful productions are due to my own inadequacies in that particular field or due to other circumstances.

If you didn't have a flexible theatre, such as you have, The Questors Theatre being capable of use as proscenium arch, open, or thrust stage, is there any one form of theatre that you feel lends itself satisfactorily to the majority of productions?

As you know I'm very keen on the flexible theatre and worked to create one here at Ealing. If I were told, 'You can only have one form, so which form is the one that is most generally used for all kinds of plays?' – then I think I would say a thrust stage. If I were setting out to create another theatre for myself I am very inclined to think I would have a very simple theatre in-the-round. I find the challenge of that very exciting and when I've seen it work it seems to work extraordinarily well. But there are some plays that are a little difficult to achieve in-the-round.

Quite a good case in point was when I did *Uncle Vanya*. I did that in-the-round and I thought that worked very well. There was only one purely technical practical problem and that was the map of Africa in the last act. I substituted for the map of Africa a globe of the world. Not as satisfactory as a map of Africa, but it worked reasonably and it was a small price to pay for all the other advantages of being able to do it in-the-round. When I tackled *Three Sisters* I realized it really was not practicable to do that in-the-round, because in the first act you must have the counterpoint between what's really basically the drawing room in the front and the dining room at the back with the counterpoint of characters in one with the other. This couldn't work in-the-round, because for part of the audience one stage would be in the foreground and the other one in the background, but for the other part of the audience that would be reversed and they would get a totally different picture of the play in consequence; so I don't think for that reason that *Three Sisters* would work in-the-round. So there are plays which don't really work as well in-the-round. Theatres in-the-round, of course, have been working for years and years and years and don't really seem to have any insuperable problems.

Do you, like Helen Mirren in her letter to the press some time ago, feel that the technical side of theatre – computerized lighting, scene shifting, music, effects, cues and elaborate costuming – militate against the relationship of the actor and his audience?

Personally, I am inclined to think so, but I think it depends upon what kind of theatre you want. If you want theatre of spectacle all these things are quite important and that's what you go to see and you need gorgeous costumes and transformation scenes and super lighting and fantastic sound effects and so on. And if that's going to be achieved then technical improvements to make it better are a good thing. It just happens that's not the theatre that appeals most to me personally. I like a theatre that is for hearing and sharing with the actors what they are bringing to life on the stage and for that kind of theatre too much spectacle rather gets in the way. And of course the more elaborate, the more complicated, the more finished all the technical possibilities are the more people want to use them and there is a tendency in that direction. I have often felt this in shows that I've seen in some of the more prestigious theatres, such as the National, in which one would have liked a much simpler presentation, where one could really share with the actors to a greater degree. I think it depends upon what one, personally, wants from the theatre. One can enjoy a spectacle from time to time too, of course.

What sort of experience do you feel would be most useful to a potential director?

I think this is a very difficult question to answer in a clear way. Obviously anyone who is going to direct needs experience of all aspects of the theatre. He may sometimes have to have theatre in his blood. I think that experience as an actor is really quite important to a director, because, it seems to me, that what a director is doing is working with the actor in the actor's own imagination, as it were. If he hasn't experienced acting he doesn't understand how the actor works – even understanding the kinds of personal blocks an actor can have that make some things difficult for him. So I would have thought that experience of acting is perhaps one of the most important things, but any kind of theatre experience is valuable. One has to widen one's whole experience of theatre by visiting theatres of all kinds. Also widen one's experience of life, by being aware of people – what makes people tick and so on, which is what an actor has to do. If you are suggesting that there is some specific kind of key or course or training, which is essential and would do the trick, I don't think that is so, but that does not mean that a director can't learn a great deal about his actual job. I think there are far too many directors about in the professional, as well as the amateur theatre, who simply don't know their job.

DAVID KELSEY

David Kelsey is the Artistic Director of the Royal Theatre, Northampton. He has lectured and directed all over the world and is the author of several plays. He is currently Artistic Director for the Ludlow Shakespeare Season.

What sort of theatre experience did you have before you commenced directing?

9 The Théâtre du Soleil's Paris production of *1789*. The action took place on five rostra, around which the audience sat, stood or wandered at will.

10 A production of *Chinchilla* by Robert David MacDonald at the Glasgow Citizens, 1977. An example of very sparse staging lending an elegance and power to the actor on the stage. The deployment of the cast in depth, breadth and elevation creates a three-dimensional image reflecting tensions between characters. The design is by Phillip Prowse.

11 Peter Brook's 1970 Stratford production of *A Midsummer Night's Dream.* In the plain white setting, by Sally Jacobs, movement gained a special significance. The acting area was fully used as a three-dimensional space, with Titania flown in on a crimson bower of ostrich feathers, actors flown in on trapezes, and a catwalk around the top of the set walls to accommodate actors and musicians.

I commenced in the theatre as an acting ASM, and because I was ambitious and determined, managed to slip off the cloak of stage management and then became an actor. And then about twenty years ago I fell into the job of directing, because a director was having problems dealing with a cast, who were not responding to him. In a general discussion he asked me, 'Well, can you do it any bloody better?' So I said, 'It won't be better, it will just be different.' So I fell into directing, then I started writing. In my opinion it's useful to have a knowledge of all departments, because when you come into conflict with an author about a situation and he says, 'Well that's the line I've written', it's useful to have the actor's mental tuning fork to be able to say, 'Well I'm sorry, it may be an accurate and grammatical phrase, but it's not speakable, the rhythm of the line is wrong.'

So the basis of your work comes from having been an actor and stage manager, which gave you a thorough grounding in the theatre? And of course you write plays yourself.

Yes. Having a basic knowledge of the technical design and geography of the stage is essential, as it is the crucible for your creative work and if you know something about lighting it becomes a collaborative process. It is useful to be able to say to your lighting designer, 'Could we try this, that or the other?', naming lanterns and colours and directions – revealing that you know something about shadow and light. You make his job much more productive, because he feels that you are on his wavelength and it isn't a matter of your simply liking or disliking something.

How long do you usually manage to work on a text before going into rehearsal?

In my present working capacity it's either a three- or four-weekly cycle. Every three or four weeks we have a change of programme. In some theatres it's possible to have a six-weekly turnover. It may be possible for a director to do one play in every three-month period. At the moment at the Royal Theatre, Northampton, I'm doing one in three productions, the other two may be done by a guest director or my assistant director. I have heard to my surprise that in some theatres the director, poor sod, still has to do

E

almost every production. I just don't know how they do it.

There was a time when I first came into the theatre, you may remember this, when the resident director peddled out play after play after play in what was then called 'repertory'. Mercifully that has come to an end. The audience these days is discerning and comes to the theatre expecting to see a high standard of work. A different attitude is being taken from the home into the theatre largely on the strength of good TV drama, and I think there has been a general improvement in drama work in education, so much so that I hope there will be a deep and lasting appreciation of drama. Ten years ago that was not the case.

It needs at least three weeks to actually chew through a script and find its merits and its faults – how you are going to carve it up and how to assemble it. In other words, we have to take the jigsaw to pieces. Without that dissection in that preparatory period the director is lost when he comes into rehearsal. For that period of investigation I would like more time. I can imagine for example if we were to dig up some rare Jacobean play, or having to work on a Greek play, or a new translation, that would, for me, demand two months' work. Of course, our bosses don't recognize this. They think everything comes quickly off the shelf and you just blow the dust off a script, get some actors sitting around and the whole thing springs to life in a short time. The director has to be informed; he doesn't necessarily need to have all the answers, but it's very important that the actors should have a sense of security with him, knowing the director has a head full of ideas and the actor, too, needs a head full of ideas – then it's a question of what is suitable to be selected for use during the course of rehearsal.

Is there any routine you follow in the pre-rehearsal work on the text? Do you have in mind a series of points you want to resolve?

Yes. One looks for objectives in collaboration with the author, either present or on paper. One is looking for the author's intention. There are 'moments', skeletal shapes and points the author wishes to make. The rest is a steam-up to reach that climactic point and after that it may be simple exposition, or a slide down to the final curtain. But there may be several climactic moments in a well-wrought piece of work and that's where the director may say to his cast on that first day something like, 'I've come up with this shape, I've got a red light here and a point there, a sharp precipice here, at this point I think there is a crucial explosion, here is a positive blister and there an assault course.' The actors get those images in their minds, however they may be translated. That is a very rough outline of what I might say to the actors.

Do you give your designer a firm outline of your basic requirements, or is it a collaboration on a fifty-fifty basis, or perhaps you give your designer a completely free hand?

At the moment I've got a designer, who, fortunately, seems to reflect my own ideas. I haven't always worked with someone who was so collaborative. I would insist, in every case, that before we go any further on how the play is to be presented we should decide on one thing, and that is not colour. People can talk wild and woolly about, say, the drawing room in a play like *The Doll's House*. I had a fierce argument on that particular play some years ago when I did it – and it was silly because we had forgotten for the moment what the fundamental idea of the play was. We should really have been thinking about something like a cage, something claustrophobic. We should have discussed much more relevant things, instead of which we got into a fierce argument as to whether we should use Scandinavian blue or some other colour, and then we burst out laughing because we realized we had sidetracked ourselves and had started at the wrong end of the stick.

In arriving at a design it's often useful if the director and designer sit together and look at a blank sheet of paper and write down ideas that come to mind. This is what I do with my present designer. We ask ourselves, What are the main points? Is there a fight? Do people have to come through doors carrying large parcels? One has to think of practical things like that. Light sources are very important. One has to visualize the geography of the house, that is if we are thinking about a naturalistic interior. How far away is this house from a main road? This is important because of the window space and the sound and whether people come into a room with their overcoats on. Is there an ante-room? One must study the play very thoroughly – the designer too will, of course, have examined the script. Then the designer and director come together with their blank sheet of paper in front of them and write down what they remember – what images come to mind about this particular play. My present designer might say that the table in the middle of Act II has to be big enough for six people to sit around and have a four-course dinner, so a set of chairs of a certain period has to be found and so on. Those are just mere practical things, but it is important to get the practicalities right, because it is maddening in rehearsals to find that, say, a couple of big armchairs are in fact an obstruction and interfere with the actors' movement around the stage.

After considering the strictly practical issues I would expect any designer to go away and produce a sketch, so that I can see the dimensions, projections, recesses and the acting areas, so I can study these very quickly. Then, of course, the next thing is that he must make a model. When the model is made you may look at it and see that the ceiling piece is going to make it very difficult to light, because you can't get a bar over it, you can't get the lanterns in. So the designer may have to do two or more models before one finally decides. Some plays, unfortunately, are not as flexible as that. I want an air of flexibility when I'm working with a designer, because if you have to do the occasional West End release, which suddenly finds itself in a Samuel French paperback, it seems that the stage manager and the designer want to do all our work for us. I can understand that in the case of an amateur company who have limited facilities and don't have the opportunity of putting A, B and C together as well as they would like to. But in the professional theatre, because we have a director, because we have a designer on the payroll and, of course, design assistants, if it's a theatre of any repute at all, they would want the opportunity of looking at that play with fresh eyes. Just because Pinter's production of *No Man's Land* with Gielgud and Richardson had that certain setting, it is not the *only* way it could be designed. I was with a designer when I saw it. It was a fascinating text and the designer said to me, 'I wonder if Pinter's been as accurate about how he wants that set as he is about the balance and timing and punctuation?' I suspect he isn't. I don't think he's as punctilious about his sets. I hope not, because when I do the play I want, with my designer, to work out my own setting.

The ground plan is very important. In the ideal theatre, where I want to work, and try to make possible where I am at the moment, I think the presenting of a play should be a collaborative movement. If an ASM suddenly says in the middle of a rehearsal,

'Excuse me, but shouldn't that line be so and so,' I want the actor on the stage, and the stage manager and the director – whoever it might be – to acknowledge him or her as being a useful member of that company. I know you've got to have a hierarchy. Eventually you've got to have a referee, someone to say, 'Just a moment please, I must take a final decision on this, because the curtain goes up in three days' time.' It's very important that one doesn't over-indulge, but I do like the idea of a designer coming to the reading, because the area in which this is going to be performed is very much dependent on him. So, why shouldn't he, or anyone working within the framework of the rehearsal, come out with a very good idea?

To what extent have you actually blocked basic moves before you start rehearsals?

Well, my actual script is as virgin as the day I get it. Of course I go on reading it and reading it, until, say, a recipe begins to formulate in my mind. Now actors, of course, are invited to write down things in their scripts – textural alterations, moves, shapes and ideas in the margin and also notes, as they may be given by the director or wardrobe department, but I don't write anything down when I read a play. I recently directed *Habeas Corpus* and the designer and I got together and worked on a basic design for it. Although it's a very fussy play – I use that term deliberately – I found I didn't need to write anything down. The reason for that is that I have worked as an actor and an actor, whichever side of the mirror of the stage he happens to be on, whether he is looking at it from the stage or the auditorium – I suppose it's kinesthetic – kinesthetically you carry in your mind a sort of choreography. Now if it's written down in the script before rehearsal, and I had some experience of this from other directors I worked with when I was an actor, they are rather loath to change something. They might say, 'Well I've worked all this out and you do come on there and stand here' – for example. It's more likely to be printed on the memory as a stubborn shape. If it's left open in the director's mind he may find that his actors can generally collaborate and create something extra special, rather than be a definitive, final conclusion.

How many rehearsal hours do you manage to put into the average play, including technical and dress?

Let's take an average day. If it's a three-week schedule the day starts at 10 o'clock in the morning with one hour for lunch. Then we continue rehearsals from 2 o'clock until 5 o'clock. That's six hours a day for three weeks. It may be that the actors are working in a play in the evening. If they are not working in the evening that gives one another three hours and, as you know, we have to abide by the Equity rule that no one session will go on longer than three hours, so at the most we can get in nine hours' rehearsal out of the day. If you are in repertoire or presenting a play in tandem with a rehearsal schedule, then you're cut down to six hours of rehearsal a day. Besides, one cannot start earlier than 10 o'clock in the morning, the average is 10 o'clock, because you can only call the actors twelve hours after the fall of the curtain the previous night. It's lovely at the beginning of the season, because it means you can play around with those time schedules and get more mileage. So that's, in the normal way, thirty-six hours a week. Then we have the production weekend, because we don't open until the middle of the week, so there's all the Monday, Tuesday and Wednesday. So we have thirty-six hours for three weeks and the production weekend.

Do you usually give a preliminary talk to the cast at the first rehearsal?

I think it's better to lay your cards on the table and declare yourself to a cast – not, of course, to make any kind of lecture out of it, because actors should be intelligent people and sift out what they require. Without that initial introduction it's rather like throwing people into water and they don't know which way to swim.

How many readings do you usually have before you start moving the play?

I would say a minimum of four readings. That would take about two days – including time for discussion, especially on a difficult play: that is a play that has more substance and requires deeper analysis than a lighter piece of writing. Of course, all plays deserve as much attention as possible.

What sort of working atmosphere do you like to create? Do you favour a disciplined or a very free and easy approach?

A very disciplined approach. That may seem to negate what I said before about everyone being in a collaborative framework. I think you can have both. I think you can have a concentration on the actual product itself, so that all eyes and ears are giving the maximum attention to the main idea. But discipline is all. If you call an actor to rehearse at a certain place and time he must be there. Anarchy has no place in art as far as I am concerned. The actor's craft seems to me to be the most disciplined of all – save for dance and music. It always astonishes me that so many people want to get involved with it, considering the society we are living in at the moment. There seems to be a queue to get into drama schools and dance schools and this is an answer to some of the more pompous voices in our society at the moment saying that there is a turning away from discipline. I find that, generally, actors and dancers are the most disciplined people I know. They have to be, because they know what time the curtain goes up and they have a certain sense of shame about not fulfilling a professional task.

In rehearsing do you use improvisation as a way of investigating something?

Yes. I find it useful to unknot or shake up what may be a dull rehearsal. If two people are wrestling with a difficult patch of text and other actors are feeling a little bit limp on the side, I think it's a good idea to say to people, 'All right I know you're only playing Tom and Jerry, but you two do it.' Now if there's time – I wouldn't say it's the most essential part of rehearsal – I welcome the opportunity to use improvisation whenever it occurs.

Do you find that you tend to change moves and grouping at a late stage of rehearsal, or do you regard things as set after a certain time?

I want to be as flexible as possible. There must always be room for improvement or a change of heart – not major, but I do want to keep things flexible. You can change some things at the very last minute, but only minor things. If you happen to be doing *Waiting for Godot* you can't ask the SM to give you a different tree just before the 'half' on the first night. If you make changes it must be as early as possible – otherwise it's not fair and anything that savours of a panic measure gives the wrong sort of vibration and can be unsettling.

Do you have any personal method of getting your cast to achieve your intentions without too much 'direction'? Do you have any subtle things you say, or infer, to feed ideas?

A very good question. I'm glad to answer this one because it is something that has been levelled at me by way of, I think, praise. The immediate answer is yes. To digress a moment, because this is a very interesting question, I was on a theatre Brains Trust panel recently in the Midlands and this question came up. Because we are all trained differently, because there is a vast difference between the techniques of the RADA, the Central School, the Webber-Douglas, the Rose Bruford, Drama Centre, that is the major schools. They all have a different approach. Shall we say there's Tom, Dick and Harry in one company. Tom went to RADA and he's had a year's experience in the theatre, so he's probably worked with a couple of directors, but in the back of his mind he still carries that approach, that method he had at RADA. Now he and his colleagues – all three of them incidentally trained in a different way – are now, shall we say, side by side in *The Cherry Orchard* and they are having to cultivate a scene with extraordinary subtleties of character. One can't use an umbrella approach to those three actors. There are certain areas where they will find common ground, but I may find that I have to use an entirely different approach to get some ideas across. At the moment I have a man who is advanced in years, over the age of retirement. He is an extremely useful character actor. Now this particular actor, as far as I know, did not receive any initial formal training. Now the thing about him is that he does understand certain fundamentals, but there are certain areas that I would not dare tamper with, because I know I would be wasting my time. But I can get him, metaphorically, by the hand and sometimes guide . . . shame him into an attitude, or humorously direct him towards a line, a figure, a sentence, a move, a prop, so that that becomes an anchor for what I want and the compromise is a useful substitute.

Could you say at what stage of rehearsals you like your cast to be word perfect?

Well, again, some actors can act marvellously with a script in their hands and it doesn't get in the way. The actual business of digesting lines is a miserable process for some actors. I like the actor – this is where trust comes in – to hold on to the book for as long as he needs it. Of course you've got to watch the chap who is using the book and the prompter as an excuse for a bad memory, but if I'm reasonably sure that that actor is going to digest it and is going to give me some of that fire that is necessary at a dress rehearsal, I don't mind him carrying the book until, say, the technical rehearsal. I don't *want* a book at a technical rehearsal, because a book will get in the way, especially if you've got a lot of props to handle and doors to navigate and elaborate costumes. But if I can trust the actor I don't mind how long he carries the book.

I worked with an actor very recently, an actor I would thoroughly trust, but he doesn't like putting his book down until he's absolutely sure he's found the key. After that he might put the book down and improvise his way through it. I don't mind him doing that, because I know that he will eventually be using the original text. Now that's a very rare animal. It may annoy other actors and I say to them, 'Well at least he does know what this scene is about.' 'Ah', they say, 'but is he going to talk all that improvised stuff in performance?' 'No', I assure them, 'he won't do that.' Gradually he finds his way to the original text. I like that.

I worked for a long time with a director called Harold Lang, who didn't like people using texts at rehearsal. You had to use your own words, but never to forget what the author's words were. In a strange sort of way, we discovered, in the early stages of our company, an overseas touring company, that one got to know the original text so much better, because one was being forced to paraphrase. If an actor can paraphrase sufficiently, if he can have authority and carry the objective through each scene, by going through those points we were mentioning earlier; if he can give me the red light, and the blister, and the precipice and the car accident and the fugue – if he can give me all these things with a paraphrase, then I know jolly well I'm going to get a performance out of him, which is certainly going to be a damned sight better than from someone who can perhaps learn lines overnight and never get any further than that. The actor who has a mind full of paraphrase, which he may not necessarily use, but has flexibility – there is the actor with a range of interest.

I am rapidly coming to the conclusion that you can often see it in the face. There are some actors who seem to think they need to do some radio rep acting in the first reading and they mumble through lines as though to say it's all rather boring – we'll read it through for the director, just to let him know we can sight read and punctuate – now that actor is a bore, because he's not really helping himself. He seems to be saying to himself, in some mild rather pompous way, 'I'll do them all a favour, but I've been acting for over twenty-five years and I don't like these readings. I want to get on with the bloody job.' Those sort of actors are a bit of a yawn, because they are doing damage to themselves. If only they would open their mouths at a read-through and use their faces, however crude it may be – just bark a few lines in the face of his partner, even with a book in his hand and sitting in a re-hearsal room. Then you think at least there's someone who's going to have a go. There's somebody who's got a bit of fire in his belly.

How many technical rehearsals do you have?

Well first, of course, the stage management have their production rig, that is the setting of props, furniture and all the other accoutrements that are necessary for the play, and then we have one full technical rehearsal with the cast, who for the sake of the play have to go through the slow motion process of a lighting rehearsal, because you can't light satisfactorily without seeing the cast on stage – otherwise you're just lighting blind.

How many dress rehearsals do you usually manage to fit in?

Two, but I'd like three. I get two full dress rehearsals where absolutely everything has to be ready, including sound and ward-robe, and all production facilities have to be there to be viewed, corrected and rehearsed for the first performance.

Are there any changes or improvements you would like to see in working conditions?

All directors are going to say that they need longer time to prepare. They want a much more processed schedule for all the various departments, between wardrobe, design, lighting and the rest of the production side. From an actor's point of view I think we must look at backstage facilities in all theatres – even new theatres that have only recently been constructed.

If you can't have a flexible theatre, is there any form of staging that you feel lends itself to most types of drama?

I've worked in most of the dimensions – proscenium arch, Greek open theatre, in-the-round – and I am coming to the conclusion that you cannot live in the theatre generally without being able to construct a proscenium arch. At the Northcote, Exeter, which is the widest stage in Britain, it is wonderful to have that great space and the hydraulic lift at the front and a huge flying area, but I found that, for the productions that I did there, ultimately what I wanted was, for the purpose of set design and to focus the eye of the audience, not a constricting framework, but some form of proscenium arch stage. Naturally one wants an all-purpose theatre really, where for Aeschylus or Brecht the actors can feel a certain freedom and be in touch with the audience where necessary. I would like a proscenium arch stage that is not constricting and has some flexibility.

A few years ago Helen Mirren wrote a letter to The Guardian *about computerized lighting, scene shifting, elaborate costuming and technical effects coming between the actor and the audience. Do you feel that this is sometimes so?*

Yes. We are spending far too much time trying to streamline our activities and in doing so we are forgetting the fundamentals. I sometimes find myself doing this. I know it can be done on a much grander scale in our large playhouses. I would like a theatre with a little more improvisation in all departments and with less emphasis on the streamlining of events. I think I have a pretty good sound desk where I am working at the moment and I've worked with three very, very good sound engineers in the last two years – at the Northcote, Haymarket and the Liverpool Playhouse. All those theatres, including my own, are very fortunate in having high-powered stereo sound desks and they still have problems. We're still discovering – I'm not a technician – that the balance, this, that and the other thing are not quite what we need, so sound reproduction is getting in the way; it's taking up far too much time honing the damned thing down to exactly what you need. I certainly don't want to go back to the old idea of the Bishop's cueboard, where you dropped a needle on a chalk mark on a revolving disc – we don't want to go back to that, but maybe when we start putting a play together we should think, 'What can we do without? Do we need this huge battery of lighting or sound desks?' Somebody told me the other day at Covent Garden – of course it's a very big stage there and I realize that they are doing operas in repertoire – that with innumerable cues and lamps the lighting designer is becoming not so much part of the whole, but is dictating disproportionate aspects of the enterprise. People do not leave a theatre – I know this will offend lighting designers – talking about the lighting. They leave the theatre, or should do, talking about the play. I don't particularly like them leaving the theatre talking about the stars, or how good X, Y and Z were. Ideally one wants the audience to leave the theatre with a satisfied feeling, feeling enriched or ennobled by the experience, but pleased they don't go out of a musical whistling the scenery. I certainly don't want the audience to leave any production of mine saying they thought the lighting saved the day, because that would mean we have our priorities wrong.

What sort of experience do you think would be most useful to a potential director to give insights and skills?

Obviously to go as often as possible to see theatre of all kinds, from amateur to the productions of the large national companies. To engage himself in as much dramatic activity as possible. To read about the theatre is vital, especially the history of the theatre, because without that the young director comes up with what he fondly believes to be new ideas and we older folk have to say,

'Actually I'm sorry to disillusion you but that was thought of by Gordon Craig in 1911,' or 'Grotowski has been peddling that one around for a year or two.' I think he should eat and drink theatre before he starts putting actors together and an important thing that young directors need apart from practical experience as an actor is a basic understanding of human psychology. I think a director should have the capacity of someone who hosts a genial party with a cross-section of people. Let him, for example, imagine how he would entertain, say, a seafaring captain who's just come back from a long voyage, with a woman in the room he's trying to avoid and a woman who is about to have a nervous breakdown because her husband's left her, with a backward child who needs attention. Let him put a group of people like that together in his imagination and see if he can generate less than a boring afternoon. He becomes a father confessor, a psychologist, judge, advocate, guide, counsellor, detective all rolled into one. Actually detective novels are quite good reading for directors, because one's mind is always alert looking for the clue.

JONATHAN MILLER

Jonathan Miller, who first made his name in Beyond the Fringe, *started directing at the Royal Court Theatre in 1962. Since that time he has been heavily engaged directing for the stage and television and in recent years has been directing opera.*

How long do you like to work on a text before getting down to rehearsals?

I don't do an enormous amount of textual work before I start. Usually I become interested in a play without necessarily having a view to producing it. The main issues of the text have made themselves fairly clear to me by the time I have decided to do it. I do the main part of my textual work during the rehearsal period. It's empirical really. I go at it on the floor and resolve points in the process of discussion with the actors and thinking it out in the evening after I've finished rehearsals – sometimes reading things which have been suggested in the course of rehearsal. It's very unplanned in many ways, although I've usually read fairly fully around various aspects of the play by the time I come to rehearsal. I don't do specific homework on a play. The reason why I think a play worth doing is that I happen to have reached a point in my reading which, somehow, crystallizes the play as a topic for production.

In your lectures at the University of Kent, you said you worked from a very strong sense of visual imagery. How important is the visual image to you in your productions?

For me it is certainly one of the important factors. It often provides a defining framework about how it's going to be staged. It's either a visual image simply about the physical space in which the production is going to occur – whether it's going to be a shallow stage, or a deep one, or whether it's tilted. Then there are some very specific iconographic images which come from, say, a study of the art and historical issues of the period and images taken from pictures, which seem to me to be relevant, or certain themes, or certain ways in which the thing is structured and dressed. This will have a very strong effect upon the way the whole thing is produced.

When you meet your designer do you give him a firm outline of your requirements, or is it a collective effort, or perhaps you give him a free hand?

I have a very firm outline before I start. I know the sort of painters that I'm thinking of. I know the certain colours, tones and even the way in which I want it lit, so that we will discuss and pore over certain works of certain painters, look at them and get the feeling of the style and the stance and the particular grouping and the décor from those pictures, then we will look at certain works of architecture together and out of it we'll produce a double idea which will be fused into one work.

But as director you have the final word on the design?

Yes – one is bound to in the end.

When you start your rehearsals do you always have a firm ground plan or do you like to keep things flexible for a little while?

I have a firm ground plan and I always have a model of some sort. The furniture is often fairly movable. Sometimes I will start with a very fixed piece of furniture around which the whole production revolves. I did a production of *Eugène Onegin* very recently, in which I quite deliberately made provocative problems for myself by placing the dining table right downstage, across the front of the stage, in order to create the sense of being excluded from a room. This created a tension from which some exciting things arose in the course of rehearsals and I didn't anticipate them all.

To what extent have you blocked basic movement before you start rehearsals?

Not at all. There are, perhaps, one or two moves which I think of as crucial; certain ways in which people will come into a room, which I already have in mind before I come to rehearsal and sometimes a whole scene will crystallize around those tiny images, but usually I let the whole thing happen as we go along. But I write nothing down at all.

What length of rehearsal time do you feel is necessary for a play to develop and reveal its full texture?

About a month. I get bored after a while and I think that the actors work well under pressure. I don't like scamping things, but I find that if you let things happen spontaneously, rather than imposing things, since the experience comes from inside it happens much faster. You only have to take a long time, I think, if you impose the idea entirely from the outside and they have to incorporate it. Whereas, if it starts to grow from within them it develops very rapidly. Sometimes a whole scene can be almost fully blocked and the whole idea fully worked out in about half an hour.

Presumably this is with a fairly small cast?

Yes. Once you have large casts, or choruses, or mass movements, then, of course, you do add to rehearsal time considerably and the moving of it is a much more complicated procedure. But I don't like to block in advance. For example, there are some very big party scenes in *Eugène Onegin* and I just let the cast improvise a party and then supervised and watched it and then edited it.

Improvisation, then, is one of your tools?

Yes, but not self-consciously, but I certainly let things happen by using the creative energies and ideas of the actors. I provide them with an outline, an idea, a notion, a tone. Then having given them the tone they are almost forced to respond in the tone that you provide. It's like saying what the key note is in music.

At the beginning of rehearsals do you talk to the cast on the author, play, period, costumes and staging, or do you allow some of these points to arise during rehearsals?

I used to give long talks and I used to find that they were falling asleep. Now, I may give a little talk about the set – what it's going to look like, their costumes especially, because I think they like to know what they are going to wear. But I've become much less didactic and hectoring as I've gone on and I find I do talk a great deal through the rehearsals, but in the course of conversations we're having together, rather than simply talking at them. I find that that becomes less and less profitable. I favour action rather than talk.

How many readings do you like to have before you start moving the play?

Often I like to read it over and over again – a large number of times, so that they become un-selfconscious about the words and just simply to hear the meaning. Sometimes I don't know what the play means until I have heard it read through. The full meaning emerges from the reactions between characters. When I did *Three Sisters,* we read and read, perhaps between ten to twenty times before we got up on our feet and did it. Sometimes I have no readings at all. It depends what the spirit of the meeting is.

What sort of working atmosphere do you like to create – disciplined, or fairly free and easy?

Oh, I like a very free and easy, convivial rehearsal, broken frequently by coffee breaks and talk, and I like living together with the actors a great deal while I'm doing it. I like going out to meals with them, so that we are living in each other's pockets, so that the rehearsal period is, as it were, almost indistinguishable from the ordinary life that is going on.

So you're creating something like an ensemble during that time?

Yes, almost a family atmosphere really.

So you can create the style of an ensemble in the period of one production?

Yes, if you choose your actors carefully and you cast convivial people, as well as talented people, then they enjoy reacting off each other and meeting each other and it's out of that that it comes really. I like discipline in the sense that I don't like chaos and I don't like inattentiveness. I like everyone to be watching what everyone else is doing. I'm not authoritarian. I won't sit behind a table and I don't like to read the text while I'm rehearsing – I listen to what they are doing.

Do you tend to change moves and groupings at quite a late stage in rehearsal?

Sometimes I do, but they are usually minor adjustments. I rarely have major upheavals. The production is growing organically all the time and therefore as one part is beginning to grow you sometimes have to lop off something somewhere else. It's a continuous process of growth. Any changes are almost by implicit consent. People begin to feel, I can't move there, so don't you think we can change it to something like this? It arises out of the collaboration.

Do you have any personal technique for getting an actor to arrive at your interpretation without too much obvious 'direction'?

No. It's usually done by amusing them. I have a humorous approach to anything I do on the stage. Simply by creating an atmosphere of amusement and laughter people start to relax and to be truly creative. You create such an amusing atmosphere, where everyone is amused by everyone else, and out of that experience of creating a myth, which is private to that group, then a sort of coherence and loyalty comes from which work arises.

Do you like your casts to be word perfect as soon as possible?

Yes, I do really. It's mainly because I think that books are terribly inconvenient. Once you are up on your feet I do think that books get in the way. I am perhaps spoiled by having worked in opera for four or five years, because singers always come knowing the words and knowing the music. I think it would be very salutary if the actors knew their words before rehearsals actually begin. They pretend that they can't, because they find out what the text means by learning it in rehearsal, but I think that a rough, crude learning of it is actually very helpful. After a series of readings, of course they do have the gist of it.

Do you find that there is a genre, a type of play, that presents a particularly enjoyable challenge to you?

I know the ones that *don't* present me with an enjoyable challenge. On the whole I'm not very interested in modern plays. I work best with classical plays, Chekhov and Shakespeare for example. I've not done very many modern plays. I don't rule them out, but the ones that really set my juices moving are classical texts with very rich allusions. With classical drama you don't have to go through the crashingly boring process of reading hundreds of plays before you find something that you feel is worth doing.

If you can't have a flexible theatre, is there any form of staging that you feel lends itself satisfactorily to the majority of productions?

I've worked on practically every sort of stage and they each have their problems and they each have their virtues. I rather like the proscenium arch stage. There are certain things that I could not have conceived doing on a thrust stage. I don't like large theatres in-the-round. I think it's very hard to get a decent view. I like small theatres in-the-round very much indeed.

How sacred do you feel the author's text is?

I don't think anything is sacred in literature at all. It has become sacred by being performed, that's what makes it sacred. I don't think one owes it any more than having shown one's awe of it by doing it again. I think one is honour bound to try and find out what the author meant and not to ride roughshod over his obvious meanings, but interesting and important plays have such richness and ambiguity that it is often a matter of discussion as to what was meant. That is really what one is doing by producing a play for the nth time. One is trying to open another door.

When you know exactly what you want from an actor do you ever demonstrate what you want, as Samuel Beckett and Ingmar Bergman sometimes do, or do you leave it to the actor to find his interpretation?

I will sometimes demonstrate, if I feel it's important. If you demonstrate something convincingly the actor will often see what it is that you are getting at. It isn't that one wants complete imitation. Very often certain gestures will symbolize something, which if they can understand why you are using it, they can then reproduce. If you simply ask them to copy a movement that's no good. They have to understand why the movement is being done and also understand the phrasing of it. I don't believe entirely that an actor has got to feel the emotion which is associated with a movement. He has to feel the meaning of the movement in its connection with the emotion, but it isn't necessary to feel the emotion itself. He has to know what he is trying to convey with the movement.

What sort of experience would be useful to a potential director to give the necessary insights and skills?

He needs an intuitive sense of human conduct. He needs to be sensitive and humorous and alive to human encounters, which really means keeping his eyes open on buses and trains and watching how people behave. He should have almost an ornithologist's interest in human conduct and that interest should be carried on into other people's descriptions of human conduct, therefore I think he should be well-read. I don't think it's very useful to spend all your time in the theatre, it's much more important to read novels and visit art galleries and enrich yourself by as many other ways as you possibly can. If you get all your experience from the theatre, you will simply repeat what you see in the theatre. The business of directing plays is to introduce new themes and new ideas and the only way to do that is to constantly nourish them with the life of which they are meant to be a reproduction.

JAMES ROOSE-EVANS

James Roose-Evans founded the Hampstead Theatre Club in 1959 and Stage Two Experimental Workshop in 1969. Since 1973 he has worked as a freelance director. He has directed in the West End, in regional theatre and in the USA, and has travelled the world directing and conducting drama workshops. He is the author of Experimental Theatre *(Studio Vista, 1970);* Directing a Play *(Studio Vista, 1968);* London Theatre *(Phaidon Press, 1977) and numerous children's books.*

How long do you usually like to work on a text before you commence rehearsals?

As a professional, one can, on rare occasions, be given a script only a few days before and have to bring all one's skills to bear in going straight into rehearsal with it. Ideally, from a creative point of view, I like to know months ahead. I usually read the play many times, then put it away and do other things and then come back to it. I find that organically the whole direction and style of the production grow over a period of time and therefore ideally one likes to work with one's designer over a period of several months. One has initial meetings, one makes sketches and models – then one may, as happened with *Romeo and Juliet,* tear it all up, knock it down and start all over again. I think, creatively, one does need time.

I remember you mentioned a book of sketches that you make for each production. Do you say to your designer, 'This is what I have in mind and you can interpret these sketches as you feel', or do you give a fairly firm indication as to what you require?

I don't have any one method of working. For me working in the theatre is a pragmatic experience. It's like a surgeon doing an operation – you've got various skills, it depends upon the individual which of these skills you employ. I have a very strong visual sense and usually, when I am reading a script, I do sketches of groupings, or ideas for the set. Equally, there are times when I have no visual ideas for the set at all and I am totally dependent on the designer to bring me sketches or a model. The sketches or model may be it, or they may spark off something else in me and bring out alternative solutions. One can digest the concepts, the characters and the motivation from the text, but the actual work of beginning to prepare the production I cannot do until I have an actual model in front of me. When I've thrashed out those problems of design – then I can start to see it. Once I have the final model I play with it – like a child with a doll's house. Every day when I get home from rehearsal I play with the model, moving characters about on it, as well as reading the text each night for the next day's rehearsal. Professionally, one wouldn't go into the rehearsal situation without knowing the setting beforehand, unless it was a production where you were given two or three months in which to rehearse, which would allow time for the set to evolve. That has happened a few times. That is the way Joan Littlewood used to work. At the start of rehearsals no one would know what the set was going to be.

To what extent do you block basic moves before you start rehearsals?

Again there's no one answer. I tend to do a great deal of homework and try to anticipate every move, every permutation of movement, but I don't burden the actors with those. I think through all the problems. In any one scene there might be six or seven ways of doing it, of moving the actors about the stage.

The director must have done his homework, because then he is open to all sorts of possibilities the actors may bring. I think it's awful if a director 'ums and ahs' in rehearsal and keeps actors waiting because he hasn't thought it through. When I was a young director I used to block very tightly and impose that on actors, but that was only because I was insecure. I think that with maturity one learns to be quite open and not possessive about one's ideas.

You do block some things, major images in your mind?

Oh yes! There may be certain scenes, which are key scenes, and I may have a very strong concept and they will probably stay like that. Such as the way I conceived the ballroom scene in *Romeo and Juliet,* which was a very complex and exciting way of doing it. I was very strict about achieving this so that the whole thing looked like a Velasquez painting.

How many hours do you hope to rehearse to reach a satisfactory standard with the average straight play?

That's a question that I find difficult to answer. As you know Equity lay down a standard of hours, after which you enter into overtime and actors tend to be very strict. I would like to rehearse as long as is necessary. I believe like Guthrie that if you rehearse for ten hours one day you might have the next day off or only work for four hours. I think it's a fallacy that you've got to work so many hours each day, for the number of hours rehearsed bears no relation to the intensity of the work.

When you're starting rehearsals do you usually give a preliminary talk or lecture to the cast on the author, play, period, costumes and general background, or do you allow these points to arise during rehearsal?

I have given long talks on occasions. I remember with *An Ideal Husband,* in the West End, I gave quite a lecture before we began. I did a lot of research into the period. But I think now that I wouldn't do that again, because I think if you are skilful you weave your own research into rehearsals or encourage the actors to do their own research. You can make books and pictures available to them, or weave all this in during the process of rehearsal, otherwise there's a danger of treating actors like students and giving them a seminar or lecture, and I think that's rather insulting to them and they resent it rather.

How many readings do you like to have before you start moving a play on the stage?

I vary from play to play. The readings I don't like, and I don't think that actors like either, are those old-fashioned ones with everybody sitting round the table and giving a reading of the play. I think on the whole that that can be damaging. If I talk of readings, it is having three or four actors sitting quietly examining the text, *sotto voce,* and on those occasions we will ask questions, discuss and analyse. That might go on for a day or two or three days, before we start to move it on the floor. Then there are other plays where one begins with quite different techniques. There might be exercises, games, improvisations, or we might just start blocking it. Much depends upon the play, the actors, the theatre – the actual situation in which you are working.

What sort of working atmosphere do you like to create? Do you favour a disciplined or a free and easy atmosphere?

I think there always has to be discipline in theatre. Theatre is a complex and difficult art involving so many people, so there has to be respect for each person contributing. If it's too free and easy a lot of time can be wasted. I think you have to learn to carry your authority with ease, so that the actors don't feel that you are being paternal or dictator-like. You are there to guide, to draw out from the actors. I think the director's task is to engender a very creative atmosphere in which everybody wants to work, wants to give of their best, wants to make discoveries, to explore, to experiment and therefore everybody is working very hard, because they are working creatively and therefore the discipline is engendered by the actors as much as by the director.

Do you find that as a director you tend to change moves and groupings at quite a late stage in rehearsal?

The director is outside; he is the only one ultimately who can judge the overall orchestration and pattern and design of the production and it may seem to the director that it is absolutely right. Some actors hate things being set and constantly want to change and sometimes with that kind of actor you have to be very tough and firm and say, 'No leave it at that, that is absolutely right.' At other times if you feel you haven't yet found the solution, then, I think, you must go on changing right up to the last minute; except it depends very much on the actors – it's a nerve-racking business and some actors, if you keep on changing up to the last minute, they may get so rattled that you will undermine their confidence. It depends on the situation and the actors with whom you're working. But I think that one should be able to go on changing. Of course, the actors do need to run a production in. That is the point of previews and public dress rehearsals. If you change too much before the first night they are going to be too insecure. It's a matter of fine balance, of the director sensing just how far he can go.

At what stage of rehearsals do you like the actors to be word perfect?

As soon as possible, but again one has to adapt to human nature. I find that while the actor has the book in his hand it's difficult for him to relate to other actors, the furniture, to props, objects and attend to business. One thing that I always insist on, but don't always achieve, is to have all props and costumes as early as possible.

Bruno Santini, with whom I worked, was always marvellous at making the costumes at an early stage of rehearsal, handing them to the actors, even if it were only a hat, or part of a costume, or a prop. He would watch the actor working with it and then perhaps adapt or change it, or give it to another actor. I think it takes the actor time to relate to objects and if the actor still has his script in his hand he is impeded. Some actors are, of course, lazy, but others do have genuine difficulties in learning the actual text until they're sure of the characters. You have to sense the needs of each individual.

Is there any particular type of play that you feel gives full scope for your individual qualities as a director? Are you a man for all plays or are there plays that you are especially drawn to?

No. No. I doubt if any director is a man for all plays. I suppose a genius might be, but on one hand I do enjoy comedy, because I love the simple form of entertainment and the marvellous, but highly complex skill of comedy, which is really of course the actors. The director has less to do in a sense, because given very good comedic actors they know instinctively about timing and the length of a pause and the pointings of a line to get a laugh. It's a wonderful form of theatre with the release that it gives to an audience when there is wave after wave of laughter. But my own talents as a director are most stretched and used to the full in plays that I always think of (it may be the title of the next book I will write), as 'theatre of the imagination', such as Shakespeare, Greek plays, plays that call for an imaginative response, where the director contributes very much to the style of the production. An example was Peter Brook's *Midsummer Night's Dream,* which was very much a director's creation, with all the exercises evolved for the actors and the way it was staged stemmed from the director's concept. But in comedy the director has less to do. He is assisting. It is very exciting working with highly skilled technical actors. That is a great joy and privilege.

Is there a form of staging that you think lends itself satisfactorily to the majority of productions?

I think probably that's the end stage, because think of the Mermaid, or the Hampstead Theatre Club where you achieve the overall composition of a picture that you would get on a proscenium arch stage, but you have the intimacy of theatre in-the-round, so that there is a close physical relationship between the audience and the actor, which you don't get in the proscenium arch stage, whereas theatre in-the-round, which although it is very exciting, has its own limitations, as you have to keep moving the actors about. Also, some plays call for the contribution of the designer and theatre in-the-round is very limited in a pictorial sense. The proscenium arch stage can be rather suggestive of the two-dimensional painting. Therefore, I think that the end stage provides for either a relatively bare stage, like theatre in-the-round, or for the full contribution of the designer.

Do you feel, like Helen Mirren, that the technical side of theatre with computerized lighting, scene shifting, music, effects, cues and elaborate costuming militates against actor-audience relationships?

Yes – I quote it in my book, *London Theatre*. The lines of hers that I quote are 'that all one needs is a space, a few actors, an audience and a leader'. I think that it's a matter of balance. Obviously technical equipment can achieve marvellous effects, but I think that the most potent force in the theatre has always been the actor on the stage communicating with his audience. The actor is the most important element and I think where the actor is subservient to computers and electronic systems and grids this is frustrating and crippling to the actor. I question it. Technical equipment is valuable, but it should be kept in its place.

What sort of experience do you feel would be most useful to a potential director to give him the necessary insights and skills?

I was fortunate in that I began as an actor, with no idea of being a director. One learns so much from working with actors. One should be open to actors and willing to learn from them, because the good director is one who anticipates the needs of his actors and senses the solutions to their problems. Every actor has different problems and needs different handling, so to some extent the director has to be a good psychologist. I think that a director who is just a university man and has a too academic approach might not always get the best out of his actors. Actors are not intellectuals; they are instinctive creatures and I think you have to learn how to talk to actors, which is very different from the way in which you'd talk to students or scholars or anybody else. There is a certain kind of shorthand, a jargon, that one uses with actors. I remember the marvellous story that Guthrie told about someone going along to see Reinhardt direct and watched him at rehearsal one morning. At the end of the scene all he said was, 'Let's run it again, shall we?' He said he realized that it wasn't anything that was said, but it was the vibrations passing between the director and the actors. The director did not need to articulate. Often one uses private words when working with actors. They know tele-pathically what is going through your mind. I think you have to use this non-verbal communication. If you do say anything – what is the right thing to say? I suffered as an actor sitting through the seemingly endless note-giving of verbose directors who kept the whole company waiting, fumbling, 'er'-ing and 'ah'-ing, because they didn't know their own minds. This deflates and exhausts actors. You have to have the skill of a brilliant diagnostician, a specialist, to go to the heart of the actor's problem.

CLIFFORD WILLIAMS

Clifford Williams has worked for many years in the theatre and at one time ran his own mime company, before concentrating on directing. He has directed a very great range of work in the UK and around the world. He is probably best known for his work with the Royal Shakespeare Company.

How long do you like to work on a text before going into re-hearsal?

It varies enormously. If one's doing a complex play often you don't have enough time. I find the main work I do on a text is not so much the reading of a text, but the periods of discussion with the designer on how one is going to design and mount the piece. I find I discover more about the nature of the play – what it is about, what its intentions are – in the talks with the designer than I ever do in the study looking at it and reading it through. I'm not very good at just reading the text. I find it a bit boring at times – just reading through a play time and time again. Nevertheless I suppose one would hope to have, before one goes to the first re-hearsal, a period of perhaps five or six weeks. At the beginning of that six-week period one reads the play for the first time and cogitates a bit and meets the author and a few changes are made; a fortnight's gone by and one now meets the designer and talks with him. He designs the set. That usually takes about three or four weeks and that brings you to the first rehearsal. So it's usually spread over about six weeks, sometimes a little longer. If it were not a new play, but an established play – a classic play – probably slightly less time.

Is there any routine you follow in this preliminary work on the text? Do you have in mind a series of points you want to resolve?

I really do most of my thinking with the designer, I really do. One works out whether the play is going to be performed naturalistically, or in some form other than naturalistic. One has to come to that conclusion with the designer, because he's got to know if he has to build four walls, or use a piece of white plastic. To come to that conclusion you've got to resolve a number of points. At the moment I'm working on a production of *Rosmersholm;* I have to come to a conclusion with the designer whether we are going to put that into a naturalistic turn-of-the-century setting or a more abstracted setting. To make that decision we do have to resolve a number of points. If someone asks me to do a production, certainly the first decision I have to make is, who is going to design it? Often I say I would like to do that production providing I can get such and such a designer and we can engage that person, because I need that designer to do that show. In this I'm probably a bit conservative. There are about half a dozen designers I work with and I work only with them. I go to whichever one seems best suited to the text, not necessarily because one goes to the one who's good at box sets, because one has a box-set play. But on the whole the decision whom one's going to have to design is almost more important than who's going to act in it.

When you have your discussions with the designer, do you give him an outline of your requirements or is it very much a matter of collaboration?

It's collaboration. A designer might ask me, 'Have you got anything to say about it?' and I might reply, 'No, I haven't got anything to say about it.' We look at each other and drink a glass of wine, and gradually a conversation starts up. If you know your designers well, they tend to read what they think is in your mind and you tend to react to odd things they say. It's very, very unscripted – not much vocabulary in it but a great deal of gesture perhaps. No, I don't lay down a brief, or very rarely. We might have two or three discussions, before he puts pen to paper or cuts off a piece of balsa wood. Most designers today do work through models. I think he's likely to construct a very primitive model and will use that as a starting point for further discussions. As a result of seeing something in more concrete terms one can say, 'Now I see absolutely, that's wrong,' or 'That's right.' He may defend or agree as the case may be and go on to another model. One might go through a series of models before one comes to the final solution. It depends on the amount of time you've got.

So at your first rehearsal you always have a firm ground plan?

Oh, absolutely. The luxury of going to the first rehearsal and subsequent to that settling one's scenery – that is a luxury that can be done by flexible and lightweight organizations. If you've got no money in the kitty to build scenery then in a way you can go on changing your scenic devices until the bitter end, because all you've got are chairs and minor items. But if you're in a heavier situation – that is, within a conventional theatre situation where you've got to spend money on your scenery and you can't make do with agitprops – when you are in that situation you do have to say, 'Well that's the set and that's what we're sticking with.' You cannot change it, partly because of time. Time plus money. To build a bit of scenery to see if we like it and then build something else – that's out of the question financially. We used to do that. As recently as ten years ago at Stratford we used to try a longer rehearsal period to see if we couldn't keep some options open, vis-à-vis the scenery, until the actors had joined in the discussion. Today that is quite out of the question. Whether you are in an institutional or commercial theatre, everyone needs to know what the set is and how much it is going to cost, before you go into rehearsal.

To what extent have you blocked basic moves before rehearsal?

Not at all. It used to be different at Canterbury, when I was there. It was weekly rep when we began and then we made it fortnightly. Then, of course, one wanted the security of knowing what one was doing; with literally only six hours to block the play, you'd have to work out the moves. I used to religiously do all that, but I don't any longer, partly because I suppose I know my way around a bit more – I don't get scared by not knowing what to do next. I would have been scared then, now I don't care. Today one wants to leave it open and get the actor's contribution. But I suppose it's also because I'm not particularly interested in the geography of the show, only its inner life, and once one's got that right the moves become very easy.

So all this work is done in collaboration with the actors?

Absolutely.

Presumably you have to have your fixed points of entry and exit?

Yes. You've got that settled. I find now that once the designer has created the area, or perhaps the room in which something is going to take place, then, possibly with the designer, one has looked to see where the grand piano will go. Obviously the grand piano can't go in the middle of the stage; it has to go into a corner and you look to see where the grandfather-clock will go – well that can't go in the middle – that must go in a corner. But apart from those obvious things, and I tend to find designers agree with this, we know we may need a sofa, and three or four chairs, or what have you, but one tends to leave even the placing of those until one gets into rehearsal, rather than saying, 'Well that's the room.' On the grounds that, perhaps, if you are working with a good actor and he's playing Solness in *The Master Builder,* one tends to want to say to that actor, 'You're Solness. This is your room. Where have you put the furniture?' So he puts it around and you say that would work if it were real life, but we've got to take away one wall as we're in a theatre, so we shove the things around a bit – I tend to improvise with the positioning of furniture. I wouldn't recommend it to everyone; I don't mean this immodestly, but you actually have to have the confidence I didn't always have. One has to have the security. If one goes into rehearsal and you say to the actors, 'I don't know where the hell the furniture goes,' you can lose their confidence. The actors have got to know that you know what you're doing.

This approach, of course, demands an expert cast and plenty of time.

Of course, but a lot of actors, and good ones at that, just don't want to know where the furniture goes. They want to be told where things are and get on and use it as it's set, but others welcome a certain amount of flexibility. I think it is vital to leave as many bridges open as you can until the last possible moment – until you've made up your mind that you're going to have three chairs and a table; that is the item of expenditure you've already allowed for. You can indeed leave them where you put them until a bit later on. So, frequently, during the first week of rehearsal I will shift around the whole room – not where the windows are, not where the doors are. That's the *sine qua non,* but the actual geography of the furniture I often shift around.

How many rehearsal hours do you normally manage to put into the average play? I say 'hours', perhaps you may think in weeks?

One can work it out in hours. It depends if you are doing a commercial show, where it is likely the actors are completely free, or whether you are doing a show in a repertoire system, where the actors are performing at night. Where they are completely free, theoretically you can work eight hours a day. In fact, any actor after he has rehearsed six hours, if he has worked well, has had enough. On the whole one can say one works five and a half days a week for six hours a day, so that's about thirty-three hours for the week, and you have a varying period between four and five weeks to rehearse so you've got anything between one hundred and thirty and one hundred and sixty hours of rehearsal.

Part of the point of my question was that if under the very best professional circumstances this amount of time is necessary, then it is very important for people in the amateur theatre not to curtail rehearsal time.

Oh, God, yes! I think we have a very small amount of rehearsal time in the British professional theatre. We have considerably less than the average continental theatre. If you do have more time you must be able to use it properly.

How many readings do you usually have?

It is very, very rare that I have more than one reading. Sometimes
none. We may go straight in, having shown the model and talked,
or not, about the play. It depends on my assessment of the situation. On the whole actors say they don't like first readings, it
makes them nervous. Really, I think they do, because it puts
off the evil hour. I would see no point in sitting down and solemnly
reading through *Hamlet*. I think it would be much better to be doing something.

*So in this type of situation, from the first moment you and the
cast are improvising and experimenting with moves?*

Yes. Absolutely. You can always do a week of that and then
reverse the process and sit down and read the play, or take a week
talking about it, depending on your timetable.

*Could you say what sort of working atmosphere you like to create?
Are you in favour of a disciplined type of approach or a very
free and easy experimental approach?*

A bit of both I suppose. It is work and one can't waste time. One
has to be advancing in some way all the time, if one is going to get
one's work done properly. There has to be a certain amount of
discipline from the company. They've got to be on time. They've
really got to try and learn their lines as soon as they can, consistent with the type of material they are doing. They've got to
keep quiet while other actors are rehearsing. They've got to be in
every sort of way alert and disciplined. At the same time, I hope
they would accept and subscribe to that discipline as fellow pro-
fessionals without bullying or shouting and therefore that discipline would be congenial, because within it we would work freely.
I think people looking in on rehearsals I take would, on the whole,
say that it looks pretty free and easy, but if they think that, it's
probably because we are being very exact with each other and
very disciplined. One can relax when one is disciplined.

Do you find you tend to change moves and groupings at quite a

12 An example of simple but effective staging by means of a ramped stage, steps, shadows on screens and lighting in Robin Phillips' 1970 production of *Two Gentlemen of Verona*, designed by Daphne Hare.

13 This photograph of the 1975 National Theatre production of *John Gabriel Borkman*, directed by Peter Hall, shows how Wendy Hiller, down right, is the focal point of the action by virtue of having the attention of the rest of the cast. Observe how the cast is positioned to make it easy for the audience to see right into the stage image and also how the linear effect, sometimes noticed on a proscenium arch stage, is broken up by subtle variations of spacing and grouping to reflect the 'pull' between characters.

14   In this production of *Summerfolk* by Maxim Gorky at the Lyttleton Theatre
in 1977, adapted and directed by Peter Stein, the characters do not freeze their
individual actions momentarily to create focal points for others, but rather, as
the Schaubühne programme states, scenes 'arise and disperse in the midst of an
enduring community'. There was a continuous flux of life on the stage to which
the audience directed its attention as it chose.

late stage in rehearsal, or does a time arrive when you consider these things set?

I think a time arrives when three-quarters of it is set and you're modestly happy with it. But for me there is always 25 per cent I am never happy with and go on fiddling with, if the actors don't get thrown, until the last possible moment. I don't actually know when the last possible moment is; it must be sometime well after a show has opened. There is possibly no such thing as a last possible moment. I go on fiddling until I'm content, or rather the actors and myself together are content. And that can take a long time. It can take till well after the first performance.

Although you did say something about this earlier, at what stage of rehearsals do you like the cast to be word perfect?

The sooner the better, as far as I'm concerned, but one has to accept that actors differ in this respect. Some actors say they like to come to the rehearsal with every word learned, while others say that's anathema, it'll come out like a parrot if you do that. Others like to learn gradually and some I know pretend they don't know the script, although they know it perfectly well, in order to keep their own options open. They go on stumbling. You think, they'll never get there, but actually they know the lines perfectly well. I don't think there is any easy answer to that. It is a completely personal one. I find the period of time when you're waiting for the actors to learn their lines a fairly boring one on the whole. I feel I can't work at full stretch until they've got over that hurdle. So the quicker the actors learn their lines the happier I am.

How many dress rehearsals do you usually manage to have?

It varies, but one would expect to have between two and three dress rehearsals and then normally, whether one's in the West End or not, with an institutional company one has a certain number of previews after that, in which you play to an audience without the actual first night having come upon you.

And these previews have a flavour of dress rehearsal about them?

F

A flavour, yes, but as people pay these days you've got to give them the best you can. We don't have enough dress rehearsals on the whole, but a dress rehearsal in terms of labour charges, staff and dressers, and so on, is a very expensive commodity and when you're dealing with a dress rehearsal, as far as a management is concerned, you're doing something that gets no income, so they tend to want to reduce the number of dress rehearsals. If you can put an audience out front with your dress rehearsal they get an income.

So you are pressurized to some extent?

Very much so.

What breathing space do you normally give your cast between the last dress rehearsal and the opening performance?

Oh, I think the time between the end of the last dress rehearsal and the first public performance, if I can put it that way, is approximately an hour and a half. You find yourself in a situation in which the theatre is dark for four days. The scenery is put up, you do your technical rehearsals, your first dress rehearsal, you change a few things, you complete the lighting, you have your second dress rehearsal, if you're lucky you have your third dress rehearsal on the afternoon of the first public performance.

Do you still light yourself? I remember you used to be rather keen on that.

No. I was enormously keen on lighting and used sometimes to light other people's shows. I remember lighting a couple of shows Bill Gaskill did once at the Arts Theatre for the RSC and one at Stratford. I lit one or two of my own shows at Stratford as well – *The Comedy of Errors,* I remember, was one. But over the years there has grown up this group of lighting designers and therefore we've started in our own time the tradition of employing a lighting designer. There are some very good lighting designers and some very bad ones. Although I would like to go on lighting my shows I don't any more and perhaps one gains a bit of time. For instance, the play I'm working on at the moment by Alan Bennett called

The Old Country, which opens in Oxford next week, is being lit at Oxford at this very moment by Glen Tucker, the lighting designer. He's been lighting it all day and I've been rehearsing all day. Of course you can't be in two places at the same time. So, he'll go on lighting tomorrow, I'll go on rehearsing tomorrow. Tomorrow evening I'll go and see what he's done. If it's been done well I've saved two days of rehearsal. But if it's not been done well, then we'll have to pull it apart again. So there are advantages about having a lighting designer to whom one can talk about what one needs and just let him get on with it. But again one would always want a collaboration with one's lighting designer, and since I have quite strong ideas on lighting, I would insist on it being a collaboration. I know, if there has to be any yelling, who would yell the loudest and it would be me.

Do you feel there is a particular type of play that gives you scope to use your individual qualities as a director, or do you feel you are a director for all plays?

I suspect that there are plays that I am not very good at doing, but apart from those – I'll think what they are in a moment – I suppose I've been lucky enough to do an extremely wide range of plays. I've done political stuff, overt and less overt, and nude revues and classical plays and quite a lot of new plays, like all the mime stuff I used to do, which had no text at all. So I suppose I'm lucky to have done a very wide range of stuff and perhaps there are some things which I am not awfully keen on doing – I've nothing against them as such, but I'm not keen on doing obvious revivals, unusual revivals yes, but I'm not keen on revivals of Somerset Maugham or Terence Rattigan. But on the other hand I do do revivals – Barrie's *What Every Woman Knows,* which is thought of as a sentimental play. I enjoyed reviving that because I thought it wasn't a sentimental play and it would be interesting to do it in a tough manner. Actually it worked rather well. On the whole I do most things. I try to avoid doing bad things.

If one cannot have a flexible theatre, lending itself to proscenium arch, thrust, in-the-round, or other shapes, do you feel there is any one shape of theatre that lends itself satisfactorily to most styles of drama?

I think the proscenium arch theatre does this. I don't know of anything that is actually imperilled by being done in the proscenium arch theatre, although it's fashionable to want to employ other forms of theatre. I've seen every possible type of drama I can think of, from the Greeks through English medieval, up to the present day, ranging into expressionist drama and God knows what, done very satisfactorily on the proscenium stage, so I don't think one can say that the proscenium stage can only do certain things. On the other hand I can think of a number of open stages on which I wouldn't want to do certain plays, so it seems to me, strange to say, that the proscenium arch stage is possibly the form that is most adaptable.

Do you feel there is an element of truth in Helen Mirren's letter to the press about the technicalities of theatre creating a barrier between the actors and the audience?

They can when they go wrong. I remember I was doing a production of *The Flying Dutchman* at Covent Garden and Sean Kenny designed a most marvellous stage which actually lifted away from the main stage of the house – lifted very high, thirty feet into the air, like a great ship rising out of the sea, and rocked and turned as well – it was a fearsome sight and on top of it was the entire Opera House male chorus singing the sailor's chorus from *The Flying Dutchman.* Thank God this was a dress rehearsal – the thing rose up and broke down with them suspended thirty feet above the stage with no way of getting them off it. That, I suppose, is the technical thing going wrong, but then I mean the most simple things can go wrong and it didn't go wrong in performance – we got it right. But I suppose because we've been moving through a period of considerable economic crisis it is natural that one can be very critical of what one thinks to be wastage. I think that is one thing. It is possible to go a step further and to say what is required is just the text and the space and the actor and that's all you need, you don't need the rest of the blarney, the lights and what have you. It is possible to say that. But I don't know how much that is the sort of theatre the audience will always want, because it seems to me that it is just one of the forms of theatre – a bare austere form of staging – but, equally, the popular theatre has always demanded its fairy lights and its tinsel and its make-up and its glamour and lots of people on the stage, rather than a few people, and lots of smashing scenery rather than no scenery. It's a question of varying the diet, I would have thought. If you've had a very rich meal there's nothing more acceptable than a bit of bread and cheese, but if you live for a couple of weeks on bread and cheese a bit of steak is very acceptable. I think everyone exaggerates the attitudes they take – it's very understandable.

What sort of experience do you feel would be most useful to a potential director to give the necessary insights and skills?

A very difficult one to answer. I think that our theatre, on the whole, is a theatre deeply rooted in the psychological realism that Stanislavski talked about. Of course, the greater part of the British theatre heritage is not naturalistic. There's not much naturalistic about any play written earlier than 1900, and a great deal that is not naturalistic about quite a few plays written after that date. Take the whole of renaissance dramaturgy in this country, it's not a naturalistic dramaturgy in the sense of the form. However, notwithstanding that, I would say in the time we've been living through during the last thirty years of the theatre it has been primarily realistically motivated, so it seems to me that what you're going to be talking to actors about a great deal is character and behaviour and therefore you really have to be a dab hand at divining what it is that makes people function and behave the way they do. You may not be able to do it with yourself, or your family, but you've got to be able to do it with other things. You have to be able to say, 'I know what makes that character tick!' and you have to be accurate about that because the actor at the same time is trying to find out what makes that character tick. The remarks you make to him will only be helpful if they really illuminate the character and he thinks that yours is an interesting analysis that he wants to follow further. Then you are animating the actor and putting him on the right psychological lines. So first you've got to be interested in what makes people tick and also you've got to have the capacity to be awed and amused by human behaviour. I think you have to have the capacity to find human behaviour and actions extraordinary and sometimes horrifying and sometimes incredibly funny. You've got to be able to take an objective view of the way people behave, not necessarily individuals, but also groups of people – because plays are normally about groups of people and you've got to have some sort of clearly held attitude from the outside towards the behaviour of society as well as the way individuals are prompted.

I suppose the other important thing is that you've got to be able to communicate with the actor. It seems to me that you can have all the things I talked about, such as psychological alertness and the ability to analyse a situation and still not be able to direct because you lack the manner, the aptitude, God knows what it is, to win the sympathy and the ear of the actor. It seems often that we have a director who's saying all the right things and the actors just close their ears, because something is not clicking between the director and the actor and when that happens, all too frequently, that sort of chap never gets across to any sort of actor. It happens with a good director, an established director, occasionally he runs into a blockage with an individual actor, but on the whole a good director, almost by definition, has to be someone who gets across with most of the actors he works with.

Understanding what life is about on the one hand and knowing how to talk about that with the actors are the two important things.

Bibliography

DIRECTING

Braun, Edward (ed.), *The Director and the Stage*, The Open University, Milton Keynes, 1977.

Clurman, Harold, *On Directing*, Collier Macmillan, London, 1974.

Cole, Toby and Chinoy, Helen Krich, *Directors on Directing*, Peter Owen, London, 1964.

Cook, Judith, *Director's Theatre*, Harrap, London, 1974.

Fernald, John, *Sense of Direction*, Secker & Warburg, London, 1968.

Gorchakov, Nikolai, *Stanislavski Directs*, Grosset & Dunlap, New York, 1962.

Roose-Evans, James, *Directing a Play*, Studio Vista, London, 1968.

ACTING

Barker, Clive, *Theatre Games*, Eyre Methuen, London, 1977.

Benedetti, Robert, *The Actor at Work*, Prentice-Hall, Englewood Cliffs, N.J., 1976.

Hayman, Ronald, *Techniques of Acting*, Eyre Methuen, London, 1969.

Hodgson, John and Richards, Ernest, *Improvisation*, Eyre Methuen, London, 1966.

Moore, Sonia, *The Stanislavski System*, Penguin Books, New York, 1976.

Seyler, Athene and Haggard, Stephen, *The Craft of Comedy*, Garnet Miller, London, 1958.

Stanislavski, Konstantin, *An Actor's Handbook*, Theatre Arts Books, 1963.

167

——, *An Actor Prepares*, Geoffrey Bles, London, 1937.
——, *Building a Character*, Eyre Methuen, London, 1979.
——, *Creating a Role*, Theatre Arts Books, New York, 1961.

VOICE

Berry, Cecily, *The Voice and the Actor*, Harrap, London, 1973.
Turner, J. Clifford, *Voice and Speech in the Theatre*, revised by Malcolm Morrison, Pitman, London, 1977.

LIGHTING

Bentham, Frederick, *The Art of Stage Lighting*, Pitman, London, 1976.
Pilbrow, Richard, *Stage Lighting*, Studio Vista, London, 1979.
Reid, Francis, *The Stage Lighting Handbook*, Pitman, London, 1976.

STAGE SOUND

Collison, David, *Stage Sound*, Studio Vista, London, 1976.

DESIGN

Hainaux, René, *Stage Design Throughout the World, 1970–1975*, Harrap, London, 1976.
Powell, Kenneth, *Stage Design*, Studio Vista, London, 1968.
Warre, Michael, *Designing and Making Stage Scenery*, Studio Vista, London, 1966.

COSTUME

Cunningham, C. W. and P. E., *A Dictionary of English Costume*, A. & C. Black, London, 1960.
Hanson, Henry Harold, *Costume Cavalcade*, Eyre Methuen, 1972.

MAKE-UP

Buchman, Herman, *Stage Make-Up*, Pitman, London, 1972.
Perrottet, Phillipe, *Practical Stage Make-Up*, Studio Vista, London, 1975.

GENERAL AND REFERENCE

Baker, Hendrik, *Stage Management and Theatrecraft*, Garnet Miller, London, 1969.

Brook, Peter, *The Empty Space*, MacGibbon & Kee, London, 1968.

Esslin, Martin, *The Anatomy of Drama*, Temple Smith, London, 1976.

Grotowski, Jerzy, *Towards a Poor Theatre*, Eyre Methuen, London, 1975.

Hartnell, Phyllis, *A Concise History of the Theatre*, Thames & Hudson, London, 1968.

—— (ed.), *The Oxford Companion to the Theatre*, Oxford University Press, 1967.

Hayman, Ronald, *The Set-up: An Anatomy of the English Theatre*, Eyre Methuen, London, 1973.

Nicoll, Allardyce, *World Drama from Aeschylus to the Present Day*, Harrap, London, 1976.

Roose-Evans, James, *Experimental Theatre*, Studio Vista, London, 1970.

Sweeting, Elizabeth, *Theatre Administration*, Pitman, London, 1969.

Taylor, John Russell, *A Dictionary of the Theatre*, Penguin Books, Harmondsworth, 1970.

Willett, John, *The Theatre of Bertolt Brecht*, Eyre Methuen, London, 1967.

PERIODICALS

The Amateur Stage.
Gambit.
Plays and Players.
The Stage.
Theatre Quarterly.

DIRECTORIES

The Spotlight Casting Directory.
Contacts. (An indispensable source of information for all requirements and contacts. Published by *The Spotlight*.)

Index